A Practical Guide to

EDP Auditing

AUERBACH Data Processing Management Library

James Hannan, Editor

•

Contributors To This Volume

Steven F. Blanding
EDP Audit Manager, Tandy Corporation
Fort Worth TX

Robert J. Coyle
CISA, EDP Audit Manager, Consolidated Rail Corporation
Philadelphia PA

William A. Emory, Jr.
Data Processing, Planning, and Security Consultant
Roanoake VA

Thomas H. Fitzgerald
Director of Data Processing Auditing
Merrill Lynch, New York NY

Ian Gilhooley
EDP Auditor, Toronto, Canada

Ben G. Matley
CDP, Ventura College, Ventura CA

Jack B. Mullen
CPA, Wilmington Trust Company, Wilmington DE

William E. Perry
CPA, CIA, CISA, President, William E. Perry Enterprises Incorporated
Orlando FL

Michael I. Sobol
CISA, President, MIS Associates, Framingham MA

David W. Syfritt
CDP, D.W. Syfritt Associates, Ojai CA

Bryan Wilkinson
CISA, Teledyne Corporation, Los Angeles CA

A Practical Guide to
EDP Auditing

Edited by James Hannan

AUERBACH Publishers Inc
Pennsauken NJ

VAN NOSTRAND REINHOLD COMPANY
New York Cincinnati Toronto London Melbourne

Copyright © 1982 by AUERBACH Publishers Inc

Library of Congress Catalog Card Number 82-11607

ISBN 0-442-20909-6

All rights reserved. No part of this work covered by the copyright hereon may be reproduced or used in any form or by any means—graphic, electronic, or mechanical, including photocopying, recording, taping, or information storage and retrieval systems—without written permission of the publisher.

Printed in the United States of America

Published in the United States in 1982
by Van Nostrand Reinhold Company Inc
135 West 50th Street
New York NY 10020 USA

16 15 14 13 12 11 10 9 8 7 6 5 4 3

Library of Congress Cataloging in Publication Data
Main entry under title:

A Practical guide to EDP auditing.

   (Auerbach data processing management library ; 7)
   1. Electronic data processing departments—Auditing. I. Hannan, James, 1946-   . II. Title: Practical guide to E.D.P. auditing. III. Series.
HF5548.2.P66   1982   657'.453   82-11607
ISBN 0-442-20909-6 (pbk.)

Contents

Preface vii

Introduction ix

Chapter 1 Defining EDP Audit Objectives
           William A. Emory, Jr. 1

2 Defining the Scope of DP Controls
   Ian Gilhooley 15

3 Writing EDP Audit Reports
   William E. Perry 33

4 Auditing DP Standards
   Ben G. Matley & David W. Syfritt 45

5 Test Design for Systems under Development
   Jack B. Mullen 59

6 Applications Projects Cost/Benefit Review
   Bryan Wilkinson 83

7 Auditing Application Programs
   Michael I. Sobol 99

8 Auditing an MVS Operating System
   Robert J. Coyle 107

9 The Auditor's Use and Control of Utility
   Programs
   Michael I. Sobol 119

10 Auditing JCL Standards
   Steven F. Blanding 129

11 Auditing Minicomputer-Based Systems
   Thomas H. Fitzgerald 139

Contents

12 Hardware Acquisition Cost/Benefit Review
Bryan Wilkinson 151

Preface

In its relatively brief existence, the computer has emerged from the back rooms of most organizations to become an integral part of business life. Increasingly sophisticated data processing systems are being used today to solve increasingly complex business problems. As a result, the typical data processing function has become as intricate and specialized as the business enterprise it serves.

Such specialization places a strenuous burden on computer professionals. Not only must they possess specific technical expertise, they must understand how to apply their special knowledge in support of business objectives and goals. A computer professional's effectiveness and career hinge on how ably he or she manages this challenge.

To assist computer professionals in meeting this challenge, AUERBACH Publishers has developed the *AUERBACH Data Processing Management Library*. The series comprises eight volumes, each addressing the management of a specific DP function:

A Practical Guide to Data Processing Management
A Practical Guide to Programming Management
A Practical Guide to Data Communications Management
A Practical Guide to Data Base Management
A Practical Guide to Systems Development Management
A Practical Guide to Data Center Operations Management
A Practical Guide to EDP Auditing
A Practical Guide to Distributed Processing Management

Each volume contains well-tested, practical solutions to the most common and pressing set of problems facing the manager of that function. Supplying the solutions is a prominent group of DP practitioners—people who make their living in the areas they write about. The concise, focused chapters are designed to help the reader directly apply the solutions they contain to his or her environment.

AUERBACH has been serving the information needs of computer professionals for more than 25 years and knows how to help them increase their effectiveness and enhance their careers. The *AUERBACH Data Processing Management Library* is just one of the company's many offerings in this field.

James Hannan
Assistant Vice President
AUERBACH Publishers

Introduction

In less than two generations, the computer has profoundly altered the structure and functions of most organizations. In some cases, the computer has helped to create sleeker organizational structures and more efficient modes of operation; in others, it has served to buttress outmoded forms and to institutionalize cumbersome processes. In all cases, however, the computer has rendered obsolete traditional methods of verifying and controlling the typical organization's data and procedures. Unfortunately, many enterprises have been slow to adopt the forms of control required in this new environment.

Although several factors have contributed to this lag, two are especially significant: the technical complexity of modern computer systems and the "mind set" of those who build and run them. The average medium to large system is an engineering marvel, with powerful high-speed hardware, sophisticated firmware and systems software, and complex and idiosyncratic application programs. The systems are designed, configured, and operated by technicians who, understandably, are more concerned with processing speed and technical "elegance" than with verification and control.

In response to this situation, many organizations have established an EDP auditing function and have attempted to staff it with people who know as much about computers as they do about principles of control. Finding such people, however, has not been easy: because the function is relatively new, experienced auditors are scarce. What is more, few educational institutions offer extensive EDP auditing curricula. Thus even the best-intentioned organizations have been unable to keep pace with computerization in their attempts to institute appropriate controls.

The critical need for EDP auditors together with the complexity and importance of their responsibilities presents auditors with difficult challenges. To perform effectively, auditors must understand their organizations' structure and operations, as well as the role of the DP function within the organization. They must be knowledgeable about computers and keep abreast of the latest technological developments in equipment, communications, and software. They must be able to use the latest audit tools and methodologies. And they must establish and maintain effective working relationships with upper management, users, and DP personnel. This volume of the *AUERBACH Data Processing Management Library* is designed to help EDP auditors meet these challenges.

We have commissioned an outstanding group of EDP auditing practitioners to share the benefits of their diverse experience. Our authors have written on a carefully chosen range of topics and have provided proven, practical advice for managing the auditing function more productively.

Introduction

In Chapter One, William A. Emory, Jr., presents a method of defining EDP audit objectives in terms of the organization's overall audit goals. He discusses the role of the EDP auditor, describes methods for developing and organizing a list of objectives, and offers suggestions for gaining management support for the objectives.

Although the introduction of data processing did not change the objectives of internal control, it did alter the methods for achieving those objectives. In his "Defining the Scope of DP Controls," Ian Gilhooley describes the controls that should be present in this new environment.

In addition to well-defined objectives, the effectiveness of an EDP audit depends on whether the recommendations included in the audit report are accepted. As a consequence, the auditor should design and write the report in a way that clearly demonstrates the merits of the recommendations. In Chapter Three, William E. Perry discusses the problems involved in writing effective EDP audit reports, describes the five types of reports, and provides tips on effective report writing.

Of all the areas with which the EDP auditor must be concerned, perhaps the most fundamental is that of DP standards. Such standards are crucial to maintaining control over DP applications. In addition, the absence or neglect of standards can hinder the effectiveness of traditional control in non-DP areas. In Chapter Four, Ben G. Matley and David W. Syfritt provide a step-by-step procedure for determining the existence and effectiveness of DP standards.

An activity in which DP standards are particularly important is systems development. Although there is no general agreement on the extent of audit activities during the systems development life cycle, the auditor should take part in this process to ensure the adequacy of internal control systems. To do this, the auditor must examine two major areas: internal controls over the computer and manual systems and administrative controls over the systems development process. In his "Test Design for Systems under Development," Jack B. Mullen presents a checklist for in-depth auditor involvement in the systems development process.

After major systems have been developed, the auditor should conduct post-implementation audits to determine the accuracy of cost/benefit estimates made before the start of the projects. These reviews are necessary because management bases decisions about applications projects on those estimates. In Chapter Six, Bryan Wilkinson describes how to conduct a cost/benefit review of applications projects.

The source code of application programs should also be audited. Although source code analysis is time consuming and requires a great deal of technical skill, the potential benefits make it a productive and informative activity. In Chapter Seven, Michael I. Sobol discusses various methods and tools useful in auditing application programs.

Introduction

In addition to application programs, the EDP auditor must be familiar with operating systems, utility programs, and job control languages (JCLs). Operating systems are programs (or sets of programs) that direct the activities of computers; they are the "brain" of any computer system. Utility programs are powerful and convenient tools for performing redundant tasks in the data center. Their capabilities make them both useful and a security risk. JCL is a high-powered, flexible language used to define the tasks performed by the computer and thus should be subject to strict standards. In Chapter Eight, Robert J. Coyle presents a systematic approach to reviewing a particular operating system—the IBM Multiple Virtual Storage (MVS) operating system. This is followed by Michael I. Sobol's discussion of the auditor's use and control of utility programs in Chapter Nine. And in Chapter Ten, Steven F. Blanding describes how JCL standards are enforced and how the auditor can approach their review.

The proliferation of minicomputers has added a new level of complexity to the auditor's tasks. Because the degree of control inherent in large-scale systems is often absent in minis, the auditor must develop a workable audit plan that takes into account the unique nature of these devices; he or she must also find alternate methods to accomplish audit objectives. In Chapter Eleven, Thomas H. Fitzgerald presents control techniques that can minimize the risks posed by minicomputers.

Post-installation cost/benefit review of hardware acquisitions may not be considered part of the EDP auditor's bailiwick in most organizations. As one who monitors the use of company assets, however, the auditor should recommend a thorough and impartial follow-up of hardware acquisition projects. Bryan Wilkinson describes such a review in Chapter Twelve.

1 Defining EDP Audit Objectives

by William A. Emory, Jr.

INTRODUCTION

Many articles have been written concerning the EDP auditor's role—as viewed by the general auditor, the EDP manager, and by senior management. Although this type of article provides useful information, it leaves unanswered such questions as:
- What is the proper role of the EDP auditor?
- What are the objectives of EDP auditing?
- How can these objectives be defined?

Another problem in defining EDP audit objectives is illustrated by the following examples. At one large wholesale distributor, the internal audit procedures for accounts receivable include the following instruction: Verify the totals on the computer output to the departmental or general ledger controls. After this instruction, the financial auditors routinely placed the following comment: Performed by EDP auditors. A subsequent review of the EDP audit procedures revealed that the EDP auditor had no procedure for verifying computer output to user controls. Each had simply assumed that the other was responsible for this procedure.

In a banking institution, the financial auditors developed a program in which they used their calculators to verify interest calculations on consumer loans during their annual audit of the consumer loan department. In this same organization, the EDP auditor conducted periodic application reviews. One objective was to test the accuracy of program documentation. The method involved using the documented interest calculations in an audit software program to recalculate the loan interest and then comparing these figures with the interest calculated by the production program. In this case, although the two audit groups had different audit objectives, there was a clear duplication of effort.

Unfortunately, these are not isolated, or even unusual, cases. Important audit objectives are missed and effort duplicated because audit objectives are not clearly defined and because responsibility for these objectives is not definitively assigned.

To avoid these problems, the role of the EDP auditor must be defined in terms of the objectives of EDP auditing, and the objectives of EDP auditing must be defined in terms of the overall audit goals of the individual organization.

THE ROLE OF THE EDP AUDITOR

The proper role for an EDP auditor is the one that most effectively contributes to the organization's total audit needs. Although no article, portfolio, or book on EDP auditing can define exactly what the auditor's role or specific objectives should be, published sources can provide excellent guidelines and useful ideas. When developing role definition and audit objectives, the EDP auditor should consider the following:

- The structure and goals of the organization in which he or she works
- The characteristics of the DP department
- The needs and objectives of the financial auditors
- His or her own capabilities and those of the EDP audit staff

The Organization. The organizational structure, the levels at which DP and auditing report, the management philosophy, the corporate goals, and even the product lines all have some influence on defining the EDP audit objectives. For example, in the banking industry the computer applications are an integral part of the product line (financial services), and the computer operation, or at least the output, is highly visible to the customer. In this situation, application auditing receives high priority as an EDP audit objective. A computer service bureau, however, may process many customer applications, but the service contract may specify that the customer has responsibility for auditing the application. In this case, application auditing would not be an appropriate objective for the EDP auditor.

The DP Department. The general makeup and relative sophistication of the data center must be considered when defining EDP audit objectives. For example, the EDP auditor responsible for a multisite data center that has online processing and an extensive data communications network has different objectives than does the auditor for a single-site center with all batch processing. Ensuring that adequate controls are incorporated during systems design might be an excellent objective in a center that develops new systems but may be inappropriate for a turnkey operation that uses only vendor-supplied software.

Financial Audit Objectives. If the financial records of the organization are highly automated and the financial auditors have little DP background, the most efficient role for the EDP auditor may be to provide support for the financial auditors. Another important objective might be to provide basic DP training for the financial auditors.

The specific audit objectives of the financial auditors must also be carefully considered. Coordinating the functions of both auditing groups helps

DEFINING AUDIT OBJECTIVES

eliminate duplication and avoid oversights. For example, many EDP auditors review DP personnel policies and evaluate employee performance. Financial auditors may review general personnel policy for the entire company and may evaluate the performance of key personnel. Coordination of audit objectives between the two groups can eliminate duplication of effort in this area.

EDP Auditor Capabilities. Another factor that must be considered in setting EDP audit objectives is the capability—training and experience—of the EDP auditors. It makes little sense to set objectives that the auditors are incapable of attaining. Once the objectives are defined, the beneficiaries of the audit (e.g., senior management and the board of directors) have every right to hold the auditors responsible for meeting those objectives. It is therefore more prudent to leave unspecified those objectives that the auditors cannot attain.

This course of action may create a dilemma for the EDP auditor. If he does not meet defined objectives, he is held accountable; if he leaves important objectives undefined, he may be considered negligent. Although the professional auditor should try to increase his knowledge so that he can perform additional required audit functions, the funds and time are often unavailable for needed training. A method of defining EDP audit objectives on a contingent basis, which takes auditor capability into account, is presented later in this chapter.

DEFINING EDP AUDIT OBJECTIVES

We have already stated that the objectives of EDP auditing must be defined in terms of the overall audit goals for the organization. To do so, the EDP auditor must consider every possible EDP audit objective (or at least every one that he or she can think of or obtain from reference material) and decide which of these contribute to the organization's overall goals. In addition, the auditor must determine which objectives are proper functions of the EDP auditor and within his or her present capabilities and which objectives might be better performed by other persons within the organization. Determining this can be difficult. One way to proceed is to develop a "laundry list" of EDP audit objectives.

Developing a Laundry List

A laundry list of EDP audit objectives is simply a list of every conceivable audit objective associated with DP and automated applications. When developing the list, the auditor should first write down every objective that comes to mind. Since no one person can possibly think of all of the objectives, the next step is to solicit the views of associates. The auditor should not worry at this point about whether the objectives are proper for EDP auditing; the purpose of this exercise is to gather all possible DP-related audit objectives.

This is also a good time to review any available EDP auditing reference materials. Many references are available, and while they might not specifically mention audit objectives, they should provide additional ideas. A simple review of the table of contents of this information service should suggest many possible EDP audit objectives. In addition, the list in the Appendix contains 120 EDP audit objectives that can help the EDP auditor start his own list.

Anyone with some training in formal planning or management by objectives techniques might insist that some of the items on the list in the Appendix are not objectives at all but are, rather, performance targets or work steps. Several goals and performance measurements are also included in the list. In view of this, it might be helpful to think of an audit objective as anything an EDP auditor should try to accomplish. Note that although an EDP auditor must cope with the buzzwords of the computer industry, he cannot afford to let them prevent him from clearly defining his role.

The laundry list approach should help to define specifically the limits of EDP auditor responsibility and the points of interface between him and other audit or control groups. When developing the list, the EDP auditor should have in mind one or two possible audit procedures or questions to use to attain each objective. As the auditor approaches the limits of his self-defined responsibility, the objectives should become more focused, perhaps to the point of becoming individual procedures. The idea is to determine the exact point at which the EDP auditor's responsibility ends and that of another group begins. This prevents missed audit objectives and avoids costly duplications.

Systems Development Objectives. A few examples may clarify the concept of defining responsibility limits. One controversy in EDP auditing has been between those who feel the need to participate in systems design efforts and those who believe that reviewing systems development projects will suffice. Items 31 through 41 in the list of objectives (see Appendix) address this area. Items 33, 38, and 40 suggest active participation, while the remaining items suggest a review role. The idea is to include both roles and to let the organizational needs help define the proper choice. Those EDP auditors who feel strongly about active participation in systems development may wish to expand the number of objectives in that area to help define the degree of participation.

Application Audit Objectives. Another point of possible contention between EDP auditors and financial auditors involves application audits. Should the EDP auditor review the entire application system, or does his responsibility end at the data center door? Who is responsible for user controls and work in transit? Objectives 95 through 101 address the application audit. Note that objectives 99, 100, and 101 are very specific; their purpose is to define the exact limit of the EDP auditor's responsibility and the point of interface between the EDP auditor and the financial auditor.

Audit Support. Audit support is another area that must be defined. How much and what types of support does the EDP audit staff provide for the financial audit staff? Who is responsible for developing audit software for use

DEFINING AUDIT OBJECTIVES 5

in conducting financial audits? Objectives 112 through 120 cover the area of audit support. Objective 115, which relates to reconciling automated output, is always a disputed issue. While many EDP auditors think this task beneath their dignity, many financial auditors believe that reconciling output is the only valid reason for having EDP auditors. Although this chapter cannot resolve this conflict, it does recommend that this objective be specifically included in the list. The EDP auditor should also include any other items that he feels he should not be responsible for, even though the items are DP related. The purpose of the list is to define the auditor's role based on the needs of the organization; this may include accepting responsibility for some objectives that he feels belong to someone else.

Objectives beyond Present Capabilities. Mentioned earlier were the problems involved with defining objectives beyond the auditor's present capabilities. Items 76 and 80, which relate to telecommunications, are examples of objectives for which many EDP auditors feel unqualified. At this point in the development of the list, this type of objective should be included, regardless of the staff's ability to accomplish such objectives.

Organizing the List

The next step is to meaningfully organize the list, remembering that people outside the EDP audit staff who may lack a background in either DP or auditing will review it.

When organizing the list, the first step is to eliminate any objectives that do not apply to the DP operation in the organization. For example, if the organization does not have a data communications network, items 76 through 81 should be omitted. If there is no systems development work done in the organization, objectives 31 through 41 should be omitted. The idea is to keep the list as short as possible, while covering all bases. When editing the list and eliminating possible objectives, the auditor should note the reason he is omitting them.

Lists of audit objectives are generally organized in the same format as are the procedures used to conduct the audits (i.e., audit objectives and audit procedures should parallel each other). The audit procedures themselves are usually organized in order of control objectives (audit goals). Control objectives are broad audit objectives, such as:
- Ensure the integrity of the data being processed.
- Prevent unauthorized access to information.
- Ensure the continued availability of the computer resources.

Based on this type of organization, most EDP auditors conduct audits of such items as data integrity, physical security, logical access security, and emergency preparedness.

Although these categories are valid as broad objectives for the EDP auditor, they are too broad to be auditable, as they overlap too many functional lines within DP. Each individual function contributes something toward these goals, but none totally covers any of them. As an alternative, the audit objectives should be arranged into DP functional areas based on the organization of the DP operations within the company.

Figure 1-1 shows an organizational chart for a typical medium-sized DP operation. Based on this chart, Table 1-1 gives a laundry list of objectives broken down into DP functional areas.

Organizing the list of objectives by DP functional area has several advantages. An EDP auditor should be aware of the work that is performed in each area and how it relates to the overall DP effort; this type of organization may thus help him think of additional objectives or audit procedures. Management at all levels is more accustomed to thinking in terms of organizational structure than in terms of control objectives; a functional approach should thus more clearly delineate the objectives to management. This arrangement also helps management to suggest additional objectives or to spot objectives that may have been included in the wrong functional area.

By arranging the objectives into functional areas, the auditor should be able to develop the audit procedures into functional audit units. This can help improve the control over EDP audit performance by creating smaller, better-defined audit units. It should also help improve the auditor/auditee relationship by limiting individual audits to specifically defined functions and groups of employees.

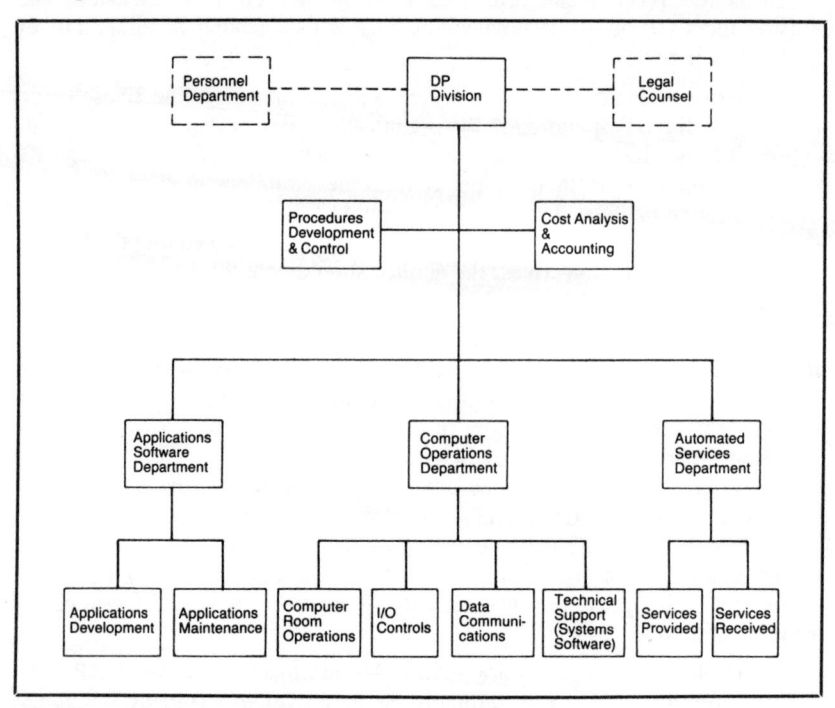

Figure 1-1. Organizational Chart

DEFINING AUDIT OBJECTIVES

Table 1-1. EDP Audit Objectives Arranged by DP Function

I. **Administrative**
   A. Organizational and Personnel—Objectives 1 through 8
   B. Planning—Objectives 9 through 13
   C. Cost Analysis and Accounting—Objectives 14 through 17
   D. Procedures Development and Control—Objectives 18 through 23
   E. Legal Matters—Objectives 24 through 28

II. **Application Systems and Programming**
   A. Application Software Development—Objectives 29 through 41
   B. Application Software Maintenance—Objectives 42 through 50

III. **Computer Operations Department**
   A. Computer Room Operations—Objectives 51 through 69
   B. I/O Controls—Objectives 70 through 74
   C. Data Communications—Objectives 75 through 81
   D. Technical Support—Objectives 82 through 87

IV. **Automated Services**
   A. Services Provided—Objectives 88 through 92
   B. Services Received—Objectives 93 and 94

V. **Automated Applications**—Objectives 95 through 111 (for each existing production application)

VI. **Audit Support**—Objectives 112 through 120

Distributing the List

After the list is trimmed down and properly organized, it is ready for distribution. It should be distributed to those persons directly responsible for, or interested in, the EDP audit function. The distribution list should include the Corporate Auditor (Audit Manager), the Director of DP (Data Center Manager), the Senior Operations Officer (the person to whom the Director of DP reports), and the Audit Committee of the Board of Directors (if such a committee exists).

The audit objectives cannot be distributed without some instructions to the recipients. These instructions should be written and should include a brief statement of purpose. In addition, they should request the recipient to review the list and to indicate whether he thinks each item is a proper objective for the EDP auditor. If the recipient disagrees with an objective, he should give a reason. He should also include any additional objectives that he feels would be worthwhile. The instructions should include a time limit for returning the lists.

In addition to written instructions, the EDP auditor should try to hand deliver the lists and should be prepared to give a short oral presentation to each recipient. The presentation should emphasize the importance of the list and the necessity for a candid and thoughtful response. Of course, the EDP auditor should be available to answer any questions.

Potential Problems

Three potential problems regarding those who review the lists of objectives should be anticipated. First, senior management often takes a rubber-stamp approach to such a review. They may not understand the list nor have time to find out more about it. Instead, they simply approve and return it. When this happens, nothing is really accomplished.

The second problem, usually associated with DP management and the financial audit staff, is the "that's a good idea—do it" approach. An objective may be considered worthwhile, but some question over where or by whom the objective should be done may remain. Since it entails procedures that no one really enjoys doing, the person reviewing the list takes the easy way out and simply lets the EDP auditor do it. This is only slightly better than the rubber-stamp review. In this situation, EDP audit objectives may have been thoughtfully defined, but the auditor cannot depend on whether they have been coordinated with the overall audit and management control objectives of the organization.

The third potential problem involves EDP auditor capabilities or lack thereof. This chapter stated earlier that worthwhile objectives should be included, even if the EDP audit staff lacks the capability to perform the procedures dictated by the objectives. If the reviewers of the list conclude that these are worthwhile objectives and should be the responsibility of the EDP auditor, that auditor may be in a real bind. He has a clear mandate but is unable to perform the required tasks. If the auditor asks management for more training in order to meet the objectives, he may lose credibility or may even be accused of using underhanded methods to justify more training.

If the auditor feels that these or similar problems apply to his organization, he should address them before distributing the list of objectives. One approach would be to emphasize the potential problems in the written and oral instructions. Perhaps a better approach is to divide the list into three sections. The first part would include the objectives that the EDP auditor feels are worthwhile and that he should perform. The second part would list objectives that the auditor feels are worthwhile but that should be performed by someone other than EDP audit staff members. The third part of the list would contain objectives that the auditor considers worthwhile but beyond the present capabilities of the EDP audit staff (a brief explanation of the reason the objective is beyond current audit capabilities should probably be included).

In addition to the three-part approach, the use of a form may help overcome some of the potential problems. A clearly organized form often helps accelerate the review process by immediately focusing the reviewer's attention on the more important issues. Figure 1-2 shows such a form.

These methods should help overcome the potential problems. If the auditor gets a rubber-stamp response, at least he knows that the reviewer considered his viewpoint. If he is mandated to perform beyond the present capabilities of the audit staff, he has a good case for the needed training.

DEFINING AUDIT OBJECTIVES

Objective	OK? Yes	OK? No	Comments

I. Administrative
A. Organizational and Personnel
  1. Review organizational chart for adequacy of staffing, separation of duties, and so on.
  2. Test actual structure for compliance with defined organization.			

Figure 1-2. Sample EDP Audit Objectives Form

The Final List

After performing the various exercises described in this chapter, the auditor should end up with several lists of objectives, each with the viewpoints and recommendations of different levels of management who are concerned with both audit and DP. The final task is to combine these lists into one working list that defines the specific objectives for EDP audit activities.

Combining the lists is relatively simple. If all agree with the objective, it should be included in the final list; if all disagree, it should be omitted. If there is split agreement, the auditor should use his own judgment or take the safe route and leave it in.

If the list contains objectives that belong to the financial audit group, the EDP auditor must coordinate his activities with that group. It is his responsibility to ensure that the financial auditors understand any DP-related objectives that are assigned to them and that they develop procedures to fulfill these objectives. He must also ensure that the procedures that he develops, based on the list of objectives, dovetail with those of the financial audit group. Only with such attention to detail can he totally avoid missed audit objectives and needless duplication.

CONCLUSION

The first step in designing any system, whether an accounts receivable system or an EDP audit system, is to define the problem. The basic questions to ask are:
- Have the objectives of the EDP audit function been formally defined?
- Is there a defined interface between the EDP auditors and the financial auditors?

If the EDP auditor can answer yes to both questions, he is to be congratulated because he is, unfortunately, probably in the minority. Much attention has been devoted to audit objectives and professionalism in EDP auditing; however, there are still widespread problems in these areas.

If EDP audit objectives are not clearly delineated, the EDP auditor should attempt the process described in this chapter. First, he must obtain preliminary support. The project will take some time and will involve people whose approval and support are essential. The next step, of course, is to develop the list of objectives, distribute it, and consolidate the results. From the list, the EDP auditor must develop the audit procedures necessary to attain the audit objectives. He must then monitor the performance of the procedures to ensure that the objectives are actually being met. If this sounds like a lot of work, it is. It is necessary work, however, if the EDP auditor is to define his role adequately.

APPENDIX

Possible EDP Audit Objectives

1. Review organizational chart for adequacy of staffing, separation of duties, and the like.
2. Test actual structure for compliance with defined organization.
3. Review personnel policies for adequacy of control features and compliance with laws or standards.
4. Test personnel procedures for compliance with policies.
5. Determine that employees understand personnel policies.
6. Evaluate performance of key personnel.
7. Review salary administration program.
8. Review employee training programs.
9. Determine that DP plans are coordinated with overall corporate plans.
10. Review DP plans for adequacy.
11. Test performance against plan.
12. Determine that senior management and users participate in planning efforts.
13. Participate in planning process to express audit concerns.
14. Review and test cost analysis procedures.
15. Determine that cost basis figures are uniformly applied.
16. Review budget and budgeting procedures.
17. Test performance against budget.
18. Determine that DP standards have been developed for all areas.
19. Review management procedures for enforcing standards.
20. Help to enforce standards.
21. Test performance against standards.
22. Determine adequacy of procedures for maintaining and updating standards.
23. Participate in the development of standards.
24. Review DP hardware/software contracts.
25. Review DP services contracts.
26. Test contract performance.
27. Participate in contract negotiations.
28. Review DP insurance coverages.
29. Review application software development plans.
30. Test plan performance.
31. Determine adequacy of standards for systems design or software purchase.
32. Review user involvement in systems development.
33. Participate in systems development.
34. Test feasibility determinations.
35. Review controls on new systems before implementation.
36. Review implementation plans.
37. Review selection and use of programming languages.
38. Participate in systems testing.
39. Review test results before implementation.
40. Conduct post-implementation reviews.
41. Determine that post-implementation reviews are conducted.
42. Determine adequacy of standards for application software maintenance.
43. Test maintenance procedures for compliance with standards.
44. Review and test modification control procedures.
45. Test procedures used to update documentation.
46. Test physical security over documentation.

47. Test documentation backup.
48. Review logical security over data and program files.
49. Review programmer use of private or temporary libraries.
50. Test maintenance performance against requests for maintenance or modifications.
51. Review standards for computer operations, and test for compliance.
52. Determine that hardware is being used efficiently.
53. Review management reports concerning hardware utilization.
54. Determine that equipment is used only for authorized jobs.
55. Review plans for equipment acquisition.
56. Test equipment acquisition feasibility studies.
57. Participate in hardware selection studies.
58. Review scheduling procedures.
59. Test performance against schedules.
60. Conduct inventory of DP equipment.
61. Review hardware maintenance procedures.
62. Review environmental conditions.
63. Review physical security program.
64. Review physical access controls.
65. Review procedures for protection against and/or detection of possible disasters.
66. Review disaster recovery procedures.
67. Test disaster recovery procedures.
68. Review security over media containing data and program files.
69. Test file backup procedures.
70. Review data entry procedures.
71. Review input balancing procedures.
72. Review controls over rejected and unposted items.
73. Review output reconcilement procedures.
74. Review output distribution procedures.
75. Review standards for communications network design.
76. Participate in network planning.
77. Review network backup provisions.
78. Review physical security of network components.
79. Review communications network logical access security.
80. Test network operating efficiency.
81. Review management reports concerning network performance.
82. Review system software planning procedures.
83. Review controls over software modification.
84. Review documentation for systems software.
85. Review controls over utility programs.
86. Test utility program use.
87. Review and test production library maintenance procedures.
88. Test DP services provided to outside parties to determine compliance with contract provisions.
89. Test servicing income against billings and processing records.
90. Verify processing parameters to consumer documentation.
91. Verify contents of customer files.
92. Determine that customer processing is subject to adequate controls.
93. Determine nature and impact of DP services received from outside sources.
94. Conduct audit reviews of outside servicers.
95. Determine that users understand automated application systems.
96. Test user knowledge of system control features.

DEFINING AUDIT OBJECTIVES

97. Review user documentation.
98. Determine if users are satisfied with systems.
99. Test user data flow control procedures.
100. Review controls over data in transit between user and computer center.
101. Review application data work flow through DP.
102. Test data entry and reentry procedures.
103. Test I/O balancing procedures.
104. Review report distribution procedures.
105. Review application programming documentation for completeness.
106. Test program modifications for compliance with standards.
107. Review documentation for evidence of programmed controls.
108. Test functioning of programmed controls and edits.
109. Review documentation for evidence that key calculations are performed in accordance with policy or legal requirements.
110. Test critical calculations.
111. Verify contents of magnetic files via the documentation.
112. Develop computer programs to assist financial auditors.
113. Serve as liaison between financial auditors and DP department.
114. Assist financial auditors in interpreting and evaluating DP-generated reports.
115. Reconcile DP reports to user department controls.
116. Provide basic DP training to financial auditors.
117. Provide training to DP personnel concerning audit objectives.
118. Assist outside accountants or consultants in performing reviews.
119. Evaluate the performance of outside accountants or consultants.
120. Evaluate the impact of automated systems on financial audit goals.

2 Defining the Scope of DP Controls

by Ian Gilhooley

INTRODUCTION

Controls are individual standards and procedures that, when combined, comprise the system of internal control within an organization. The objectives of a system of internal control are to provide reasonable assurance that assets are safeguarded, that information is timely and reliable, and that errors and irregularities are discovered and corrected promptly. Such a system also should be designed to promote operational efficiency and to provide sufficient information for the auditor to evaluate the level of compliance within each organizational division.

The introduction of DP did not change the objectives of the system of internal control nor the available levels of control. Before the introduction of DP, however, functional responsibilities were defined along departmental lines, with each department manager held accountable for adherence to particular controls within his operation. With the introduction of DP, the DP department assumed many of the functions previously shared among other departments, and the various computer application programs now make decisions (e.g., whether to allow an overdraft based on the presence of an authorized credit limit) that were previously handled by a department supervisor or manager. While controls could previously be seen and physically attested to (e.g., segregation of duties and supervisory checking), the introduction of computers has forced management and auditors to reevaluate many traditional controls and concepts.

The DP department, therefore, must provide a compensating level of control to ensure that the organization-wide system of internal control is not weakened by the introduction of DP. Since the DP department is a part of the organization, its controls must be complementary to, and consistent with, controls in other departments. The DP department must not be treated in isolation when designing controls (e.g., the level of data security exercised by the DP department may be inadequate to protect data integrity from being compromised by inadequate transaction control within the user department).

FUNCTIONS OF DP

The DP department can be divided into two functional elements: the central computing facility (CCF) and the systems development department (SDD). The CCF is responsible for providing and maintaining the computer environment (i.e., hardware, operating software, and telecommunications) necessary to execute the various application systems. The CCF is also responsible for executing these application systems so as to provide the user with accurate, timely output. In addition, it must provide data security to protect the integrity of application programs and the user data processed by these programs.

Like the CCF, the SDD is user oriented. Systems development personnel must develop and maintain application systems on schedule, within budget, and in accordance with user needs.

As shown in Figure 2-1, the scope of DP can be considered in terms of the environment and applications, with the elements of each paralleling the responsibilities of the CCF and SDD, respectively. This figure illustrates the concept of the common processing environment and the multiple application systems that run in this environment. To serve the information needs of the user in a complete, accurate, and timely manner (and in a form that the user

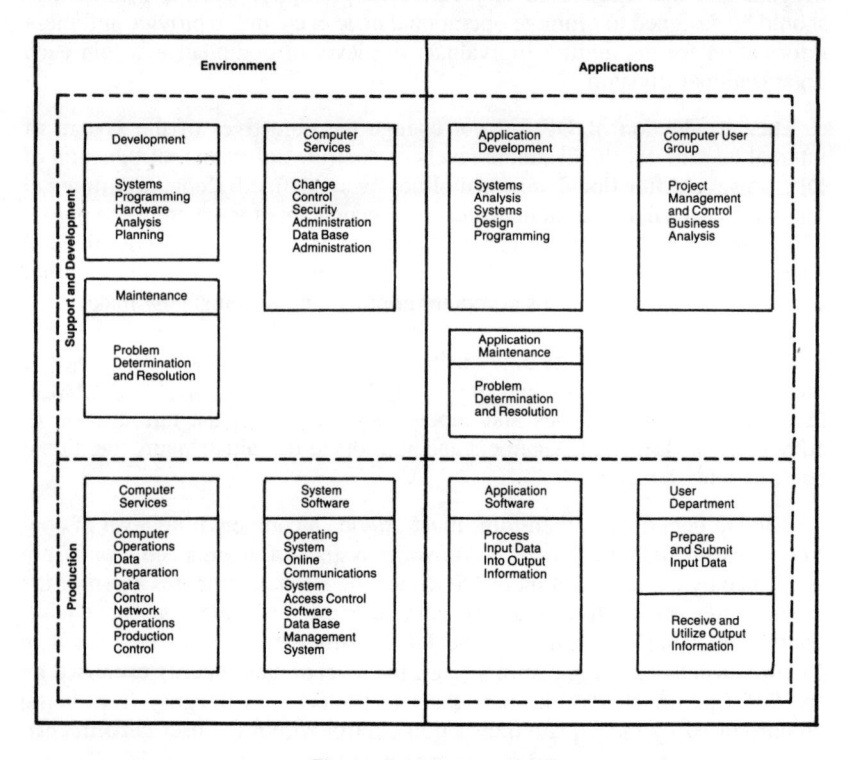

Figure 2-1. Scope of DP

DEFINING THE SCOPE OF CONTROLS 17

can understand), the DP department must have a support and development as well as a production capability.

Support and Development

The support and development capability must develop and maintain the various application systems required to provide information to users and must install, maintain, and administer the hardware and software environment in which the various application systems will run. The following support and development functions are found within this environment:
- Development—includes the systems programming function responsible for SYSGEN and for installing any other software that will be common to all application systems (e.g., access control software, data base management software). The development function also includes analyzing the current performance of the environment (hardware and software) and planning to ensure that the environment can continue to satisfy demands from the application systems.
- Maintenance—includes the activities of the vendor's hardware and software engineers, telecommunications engineers, and the organization's systems programmers. The maintenance function is primarily concerned with maintaining the environment's capacity to service the various application systems.
- Computer services—is the administrative interface between the environment and the application. This function is responsible for administering change control (e.g., promoting changes in the production environment); administering security; defining access levels to production data files; maintaining the password data set for online users; and, where appropriate, data base administration (e.g., maintaining the data dictionary and data base definition tables).

The following support and development functions are found within the applications:
- Application development—is responsible for analyzing, designing, and programming application systems that fulfill a business requirement of the organization as reflected in the needs of the user for whom the system is developed.
- Application maintenance—is responsible for problem determination and resolution when an error is detected in the application system or when an enhancement that can improve the effectiveness and/or efficiency of the system is identified.
- Computer user group—provides the interface between the DP technicians (e.g., systems analysts, designers, and programmers) and the user community. This function can exist within the DP department, or it may be a standalone department with its own reporting responsibilities. This function has responsibility for developing a business case that justifies the development of a computerized application and that can also be used by DP technicians for translation into an accurate and functioning application system. The computer user group also has re-

sponsibility for project management and control (i.e., ensuring that the system is developed on schedule and within budget).

Production

Production is the actual running of the application system to provide timely and complete information to the user. A combination of people and software functions, production requires effective interfacing between the two to produce the desired output.

The following production functions are found within the environment:
- Computer services—comprises the personnel functions necessary to provide the interfaces among the hardware, telecommunications, and system and application software. Computer services also includes the following subfunctions:
  —Computer operations is responsible for monitoring the execution of the various tasks operating in the computer; providing resources (e.g., tapes, disks, and special stationery) as requested by application systems; and taking the appropriate action for unexpected occurrences during the execution of these application systems (e.g., program abends and unexpected halt messages).
  —Data preparation is responsible for translating source documents onto computer-readable media (e.g., cards or tape files).
  —Data control is responsible for gathering the data needed to run the various application systems and for ensuring that complete output information is received.
  —Network operations is responsible for controlling the telecommunications network, anticipating problems within the network, and correcting existing problems.
  —Production control is responsible for job scheduling, job submission, and media management (e.g., allocating disk space, compressing scratched files, and deleting unused files).
- Systems software—refers to the software generic to all application systems and includes the vendor-supplied operating system, online communications software, any access control software (e.g., software that restricts access to data or library files to authorized users), and a data base management system (e.g., IMS).

The following production elements exist within the sphere of applications:
- Application software—refers to the computer programs designed and developed to provide the information required by the user.
- User department—prepares and submits input data (whether online or in the form of source documents forwarded to data preparation) and uses the output information provided by the application software.

SCOPE OF DP CONTROLS

Physical Security

Because the computer installation (e.g., the data center building, the computer mainframe, peripherals, and magnetic media) constitutes a major finan-

DEFINING THE SCOPE OF CONTROLS

cial investment, adequate physical security measures must be adopted to protect the organization from the following four levels of loss:
- Temporary and partial loss—loss of a disk drive through mechanical failure
- Temporary but total loss—total break in the power supply
- Permanent but partial loss—accidental or intentional destruction of data files
- Permanent and total loss—destruction of the data center by fire

It is the intention of this chapter to state the importance of physical security within the scope of DP controls and to show its relationship to other forms of control (see Figure 2-2).

Organizational Controls

As stated previously, the introduction of the DP department did not change the objective of the accounting control—the separation of duties. The control procedures and some duties in DP, however, differ from those found in manual processing environments. For example, with an intimate knowledge of the system and the availability of production data, a programmer can

Physical Security Organizational Controls

	Environment		Applications	
Support and Development	Development — Development Controls	Computer Services — Data Security Administration Change Control	Application Development — Development Controls	Computer User Group — Management Controls Development Controls Change Control
	Maintenance — Change Control		Application Maintenance — Change Control	
Production	Computer Services — Operational Controls Input Controls Output Controls	System Software — Access Controls	Application Software — Processing Controls	User Department — Input Controls Output Controls

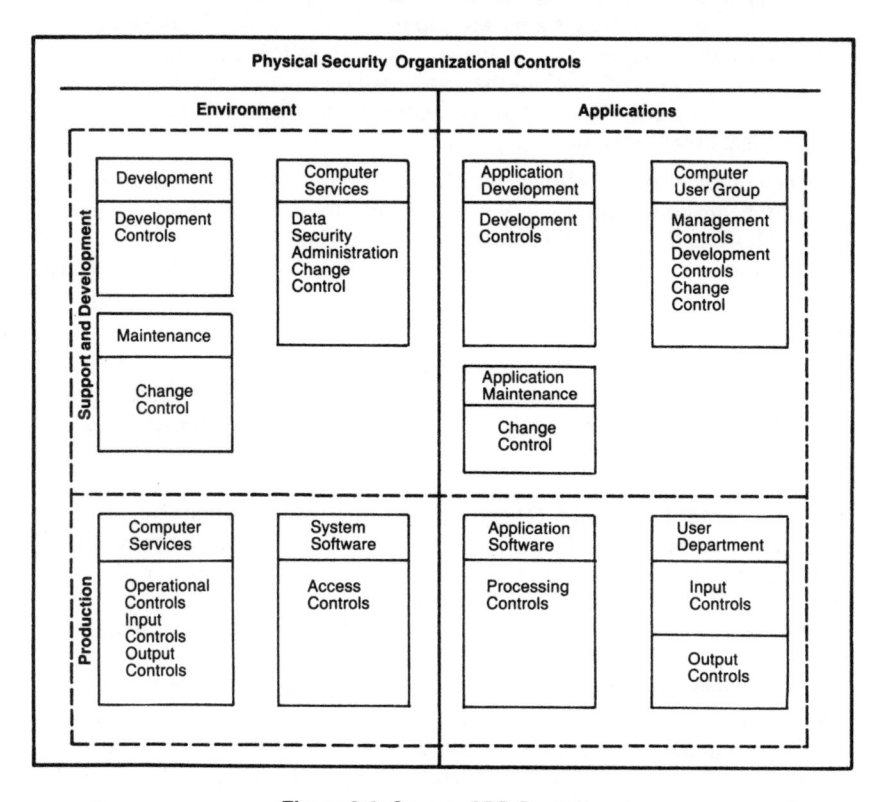

Figure 2-2. Scope of DP Controls

manipulate data to perpetrate fraud. The organization of a DP department can be considered as split between groups responsible for the environment and groups responsible for applications. Figure 2-3 shows a functional diagram of the organization of a typical DP department, based on this division. Figure 2-2 shows the relationship of organizational controls to the other forms of control.

Application Support and Development Controls

The following controls pertain to the support and development of application systems:
- Management controls
- Development controls
- Change control

Management Controls. These controls apply primarily to the development of new application systems. Management controls, which are the responsibility of the computer user group, are designed to ensure that a development project meets the user requirements. The business analysts in the computer user group are responsible for providing an interface between the user department and the systems development department. The business analyst must understand the needs of the user in business terms and translate these needs into system specifications that can be used in analyzing and designing a computerized system. He must then monitor the development of the system to ensure that user needs are being met.

The computer user group must also act as project managers for all system development, coordinating all activities to ensure that the correct resources are available at the appropriate time. For example, the user group must ensure that a programming team with the necessary skills is available when programming begins or that the user department is fully trained when the system goes live.

The existence of an effective computer user group is in itself a management control. Additional management controls include project status and budget reviews to ensure that the system is being developed on schedule and within budget.

Development Controls. These controls are complementary to management controls because they promote the development of accurate computer systems that meet user requirements and therefore minimize the incidence of after-the-fact changes (e.g., changes required to tailor the developed system to the users' original specifications). Most installations incorporate their development controls into a project methodology that charts the various activities associated with each step in the system development life cycle process. Development controls usually include review points at which management appraisal and authorization are obtained before the next development phase begins, installation standards for documentation and testing, and review of the auditability and control features of the system by the audit department.

DEFINING THE SCOPE OF CONTROLS

```
                        Senior
                       Company
                       Executive
                           |
                       Director
                        of DP
          _____|_____
         |                                   |
    Environment                         Applications
    ___|___                              ___|___
   |       |                            |       |
Support and Production              Production  Support and
Development                                     Development
   |       |                            |       |       |
Technical  Computer                  User    Systems and  Computer
Services   Services                  Depart- Programming  User
Department                           ments                Group
```

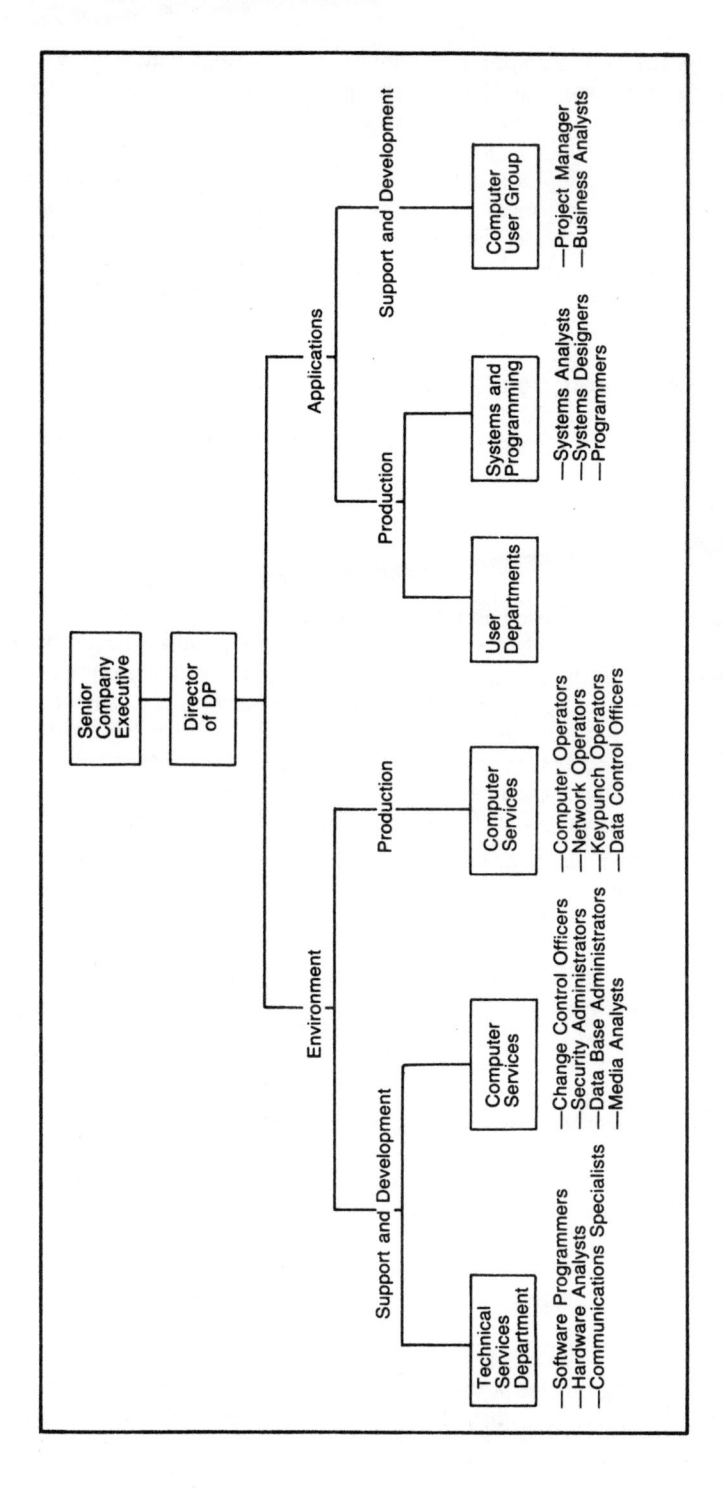

Technical Services Department
— Software Programmers
— Hardware Analysts
— Communications Specialists

Computer Services
— Change Control Officers
— Security Administrators
— Data Base Administrators
— Media Analysts

Computer Services
— Computer Operators
— Network Operators
— Keypunch Operators
— Data Control Officers

Systems and Programming
— Systems Analysts
— Systems Designers
— Programmers

Computer User Group
— Project Manager
— Business Analysts

Figure 2-3. DP Department Organizational Chart

Change Control. Regardless of how well a computer system has been designed, programmed, and tested, changes are usually required either because an error is found in the system or because an enhancement is required to meet user needs. Change control procedures ensure that only authorized changes are made to a production system and that the changes are fully tested and approved and are migrated into the production environment in a controlled manner (e.g., under the control of the computer services function for support and development). Documentation standards are also an essential part of change control because they provide an audit trail of all changes and ensure that the system can continue to be maintained.

Application Production Controls

The types of control pertaining to the production functions of application systems include:
- Input controls
- Processing controls
- Output controls

Input Controls. These controls can be considered in terms of manual and programmed controls. Manual input controls, which usually exist at the user department and the data center, include checking procedures to ensure that the data to be processed is recorded accurately and completely, authorization procedures to ensure that all data submitted for processing is legitimate, and filing procedures to ensure the existence of an audit trail. The types of input controls commonly implemented in the user department are batching input data and using prenumbered, preprinted forms and check digits.

To ensure that incorrect data is not allowed to complete the processing cycle, there should be stringent edit checks at the front end of the application system. Common types of edit checks include:
- Balancing to batch totals—Specific fields are accumulated separately and balanced to a batch total record.
- Anticipatory checks—Where specific data is expected in every run, the edit program should check that such data is actually present.
- Validity checking—The edit program should check that each field contains the expected type of information (e.g., numerical data or data within specific ranges or of specific values).
- Check digits—These digits can detect transposition of characters within a field and are commonly used for account number fields where transposition errors, if undetected, could cause posting to the wrong account.
- Reasonableness checks—Based on an analysis of what is normal, the edit program highlights or even rejects data that does not comply with the norm.

Processing Controls. Related to the update stage, processing controls are concerned with ensuring that all input data is correctly processed and ac-

DEFINING THE SCOPE OF CONTROLS

counted for. Common types of processing controls include:
- Labels—These ensure that the correct files are being used.
- Control records—These records contain a count of the number of records on the file and accumulations of specific fields from each record. By using the control record, the update program can check that the input file, updated by the day's transactions, matches the output file. The use of control records facilitates run-to-run balancing.
- Date records—When the master file has a date record as its first record, and the transaction file also has a date record, the update program can ensure that matching, as well as correct, files are used.
- Error handling—The update program must be able to handle the various processing combinations, including those that are invalid within the context of the application (e.g., an update transaction record for an account that does not exist).
- Restart/recovery procedures—When an update program runs for a long period of time (e.g., more than 30 minutes), or when files are updated in place, it should be possible to restart an interrupted run without starting from the beginning and recreating all files.
- Audit trails—The update program should indicate the disposition of all records processed in order to provide an audit trail.
- Vendor controls—These controls detect missing or incorrectly transmitted data (e.g., parity bit checking, block count reconciliation).

Output Controls. These controls are associated with the application system's reporting stage, which may be incorporated into the update program or may be a separate subsystem. Output controls are designed to ensure the completeness, accuracy, timeliness, and proper distribution of output, whether in the form of printed reports or magnetic media. Common types of output controls include:
- Labels—These ensure that the correct file is being created or updated.
- Reconciliation—This process ensures that the correct amount of data has been processed and written out. Reconciliation reports can be produced to enable either the data control function or the user department to determine that all data has been received, processed, and output.
- Quantity reports—These detail the report types and number of pages per type printed by the report programs to allow the data control function and user department to ascertain that all printed output is actually received.
- Distribution schedules—These aid the data center in ensuring that all reports are dispatched in time to meet user requirements.
- Dual custody—When negotiable instruments are to be printed, there may be a dual-custody arrangement between the data center and the user department to ensure that all instruments are correctly accounted for.
- Prenumbered forms—All negotiable instruments are prenumbered.

Environment Support and Development Controls

The types of control related to the support and development of the environment include:
- Development controls
- Change control
- Computer services function

Development Controls. Development controls within the application systems are usually developed within the organization, while controls within environmental systems are virtually always packages purchased from either the computer vendor (e.g., operating system) or from independent software vendors (e.g., access control software packages). In addition, while control over the development of application systems has been subject to close scrutiny, controls over environmental systems development have been left to the discretion of the technical services department responsible for development.

In many ways, the controls for environmental systems development are the same as those for application systems:
- The purchase of the particular software should have the approval of appropriate management.
- A feasibility study indicating cost/benefits should be prepared.
- The developed system should be tested fully, signed off by system users, and migrated into the production environment under the control of the change control group within computer services.

The main barriers to a more thorough approach to the development and adoption of controls within this area have been the highly specialized and technical nature of the business and the limited experience or interest in the area of control of the technicians responsible for environmental systems development. In addition, the control specialists (i.e., the auditors) have little understanding of this area and find it difficult coming to terms with the more simplistic application systems development. This situation, however, is slowly changing, as both management and auditors realize that this uncontrolled area warrants closer examination.

Change Control. Change control over application systems parallels change control over environmental systems. Changes to environmental systems should be authorized, fully tested, fully documented, and migrated into the production environment under the control of the change control group within computer services. The comments on controlling the development of environmental systems likewise apply to controlling changes to these systems. The topic of controlling changes to environmental systems is also coming under the close scrutiny of management and auditors.

Computer Services Function. This group must provide the manual interface between testing and the production processing environment, thus ensuring that only authorized versions of environment and application systems (whether new or amended) are migrated into production.

DEFINING THE SCOPE OF CONTROLS

Computer services is also responsible for providing the manual interface between management and the automated data security measures existing within the installation. This function also must maintain the access control data base specifying who has access to which files, the password data set specifying who has access to computer resources and to what extent, and so on. While management is responsible for specifying the access criteria, this function must translate these criteria into the appropriate computer instructions, monitor compliance, and report exceptions to management.

Environment Production Controls

The types of control related to the production functions within the environment include:
- Input controls
- Operational controls
- Output controls
- Access controls

Input Controls. These controls include the manual controls used within the computer services area of the data center by either the data preparation group or the data control group. The data preparation group may have keypunch machines capable of loading data programs that guide the operator in the types of data allowed within the various fields (e.g., will not allow alphabetic data in a numeric field, or will verify the accuracy of check digits) and that may even assist the keypunch operator in balancing to a batch totals record. The most common control within this area is keypunch verification, in which one operator checks another operator's work by rekeying the data.

The data control group collects the various inputs required by a particular application system and informs the production control group that the processing cycle can begin. An adequate, up-to-date data control manual, containing the source of the various forms of input, the media involved, and the time frame in which input should be available, must exist for each application system.

Operational Controls. These controls are concerned with the interaction among production control, computer operations, and the computer processing environment. The controls ensure that each application system is processed in a complete, accurate, and timely manner and that computer resources are managed efficiently. Common operational controls include:
- Tape librarian—This function is responsible for inventory recording and issuing and storing of tape files.
- External labels—To complement the checking of internal labels by the software, tapes and disks should have external identification labels to assist the operators when they are required to mount them.
- Documentation—An operators manual should exist for each application system, detailing the job setup in terms of the files used, amount of core required, special stationery, action to be taken on any console halt

messages that may occur, restart procedures, and any other information that can facilitate the operation of the application system.
- Scheduling—This should be performed either manually or by use of an automated scheduling package. Effective scheduling, which is essential if computer resources are to be used at maximum efficiency, is also of assistance in detecting the submission of unauthorized jobs.
- Monitoring service levels—This process ensures that the computer resource is operating at the required service levels. In addition to detecting inefficient use of existing resources, this monitoring mechanism may also indicate the need for additional processing capacity.
- Vendor controls—These controls inform the operator of any hardware or software malfunction or erroneous activity.

Output Controls. The manual checking functions carried out by the data control group ensure the completeness, accuracy, timeliness, and proper distribution of output. The most common output controls have been described under Application Production Controls. Because the data control group handles output from many application systems, an adequate, up-to-date data control manual is essential for each application. The manual must describe the various output reports produced by each program, any reconciliation or balancing required, the procedure to correct errors, and the distribution schedule for each report.

Access Controls. This refers to the logical security (i.e., programmed controls) built into the operating system to prevent and/or detect unauthorized access to computer resources.

Entry to the computer can be controlled in an online environment through the use of passwords. An operator can identify himself to the system by inserting a magnetic stripe card into a reader attached to the system or by typing in his password at the terminal. The operator must then authenticate his identification. The authentication password should be unique to each operator and should be changed regularly or whenever an operator feels that the security of his password has been compromised. There should be clearly defined controls, stipulating who is responsible for applying changes to the password data set, under what conditions changes should be made, and the procedures to be followed when requesting such a change. This data set should be specifically protected against unauthorized modification, destruction, or disclosure. Printouts of this data set should be classified as restricted information and disposed of in the same manner as are other confidential reports.

Access to data files should also be controlled. The level of access control to data files ranges from a complete access control software package (e.g., ACF2 and RACF) to no control at all. Even within installations with the most sophisticated hardware and software, it is not uncommon to find little or no security. The basic problem in controlling access to data files is defining what data should be protected and what level of access should be allowed to whom.

DEFINING THE SCOPE OF CONTROLS

The classification of data files and the establishment of the data security administration function to control the software supporting this classification are essential if an installation is to have efficient and effective access control to data files.

Although it may be impossible to prevent all unauthorized entry and access to data files, the System Management Facility (SMF) provides information for detection purposes, assuming that the appropriate computer programs are developed to report on unauthorized activity.

AUDITING IN A DP ENVIRONMENT

The auditing profession was slow to recognize the changes in the plan of organization and the system of internal control brought about by the introduction of computer systems. First, the auditor, ignoring its existence, audited around the computer. This approach entailed vouching the authenticity of transactions submitted to the system and checking that the output from the system fully reflected the input. The auditor concentrated on user control procedures and paid little or no attention to the controls (or lack thereof) in either the data center or application programs. Obviously, this situation could not be allowed to continue. The traditional auditor, however, did not possess the technical expertise to audit a computer system. This problem was further compounded by DP personnel's resistance to being audited.

The need for a person who was familiar with both internal control and DP systems became readily apparent: enter the EDP auditor. The EDP auditor was either recruited from the DP department and trained in auditing principles or was a traditional auditor trained in DP principles. The systems department now received the full attention of a group of auditors who, theoretically at least, understood the primary functions of the DP department and could develop audit procedures to assess how well these functions were being met. Systems were now audited at the user level by traditional internal audit methods, supplemented by statistical sampling reports produced through the use of Computer-Assisted Audit Techniques (CAAT), and at the DP department level by EDP auditors. Although all components that comprise the total system were now being audited, management was still not receiving full assurance of the system's overall reliability and integrity; instead, management received separate reports on the adequacy of control within the user department and reports on the adequacy of the computer system.

To gain a true picture of the adequacy of the overall system, the auditor's approach can be broadly defined in terms of the environment and the applications that run in that environment. Environmental audits have identified interface control points between the environment and applications. If an application is complying with these control points, the auditor can, with minimal testing, assume a secure operating environment and can concentrate on identifying and testing controls pertinent to the individual application (i.e., at the user department level and related to the application programs).

Environmental Audits

To assess the adequacy of control within the environment, the auditor can conduct three separate tests that, when their results are combined, can indicate the adequacy of internal control within the environment.

Computer Services Operations. Commonly referred to as the data center audit, this test is typically a compliance audit based on the policies, practices, and procedures stipulated in the data center manual. This audit encompasses the various departments and functions that comprise computer services (see Figure 2-2). It would also include an assessment of organizational controls and physical security applicable to the data center.

The objectives of the data center audit include ensuring that:
- Adequate segregation of duties exists within the organizational structure of the data center
- Physical security measures are adequate and properly utilized to ensure continuity of processing
- The data center provides timely, complete, and accurate processing of data
- The controls over the receipt, processing, and dispatch of work provide for secure processing and handling of data
- Management is provided with sufficient information to manage the data center effectively

The data center audit is usually conducted annually. The effectiveness and coverage of this audit can be supplemented between audits through additional testing conducted when individual applications are being audited.

Change Control. Controlling changes to systems is of major importance to both traditional and EDP auditors because changes represent potential exposures to the application's internal control, which the auditor has previously judged to be adequate. The auditor, therefore, must be aware that a change can either strengthen or weaken internal control. If the system of internal control is strengthened, the auditor can possibly reduce the extent of his testing. If the system of internal control is weakened, however, he may have to expand his testing or insist on the implementation of compensating controls.

The auditor, however, must ensure that a change is authorized by an appropriate level of management, tested (where possible), and introduced into the production environment in a controlled fashion. Because of the continuous changes within the DP environment, the auditor has previously had difficulty in providing effective audit coverage in this area. The first step toward providing effective audit coverage is to conduct an audit of the change control procedures and report any weaknesses or omissions. Thereafter, the auditor has three opportunities to assess the ongoing adequacy of these change control procedures and the impact of change on the internal control of any application:

DEFINING THE SCOPE OF CONTROLS

- As the change is being made—If a change is recognized as having an impact on the system's internal control, the auditor should follow this change from its initiation to its implementation. This requires the establishment of a protocol between the DP department and the audit department; the audit department must be made aware of significant changes to an application in a timely manner.
- As part of an ongoing audit of an application—The auditor has the opportunity to ensure that changes for this application comply with defined procedures and to assess the impact on the internal control of the application caused by an accumulation of changes that may not have been examined individually.
- As part of an audit of the central body responsible for implementing change—Sample testing over several systems can provide an assessment of the degree to which changes are being processed in accordance with defined procedures.

The original report to management on the adequacy of change control procedures can be updated annually or, as appropriate, based on the results of these individual tests.

Data Security. A data security audit is intended to assess the adequacy of the standards and procedures designed and implemented to protect data against unauthorized disclosure, modification, or destruction. Of particular concern to the auditor, this area typically has not been addressed satisfactorily by the DP department. To conduct this audit, the auditor needs evidence that an orderly approach has been taken to data security. The approach must be flexible enough to allow the organization to adjust to a changing environment, whether these changes occur at the application or environmental level.

The organization must assess what it is trying to protect, document its current controls, and determine what additional controls are required and whether they can be justified based on a comparison of their cost versus the value of what they protect. This audit is directed primarily at the level and adequacy of the access controls present within the system software and the data security administration procedures exercised within the computer services area. As an expert on the subject of controls, the auditor can expect to be called upon to assist the DP department in defining, establishing, and monitoring compliance with the various measures required to ensure an adequate level of data security.

Application Audits

Application audits take two forms: an audit of the application system as it is being developed and an audit of the ongoing operation of the application.

Application Development Audits. The auditor must become involved in the development stages of an application system if he is ever to attest to the adequacy of control within the system. Because the systems being developed today are very complex, the auditor cannot be expected to comprehend them within the limited time frame allowed for an operational audit. As part of the auditor's review of a developing system, a permanent file should therefore be created. The file should define the locations of control points within the system, the level of reliance anticipated for each control, and suggestions for testing these controls. Similarly, weaknesses within the system should be highlighted and any compensating controls described.

In addition to gaining an understanding of the system and its controls, there are two other important advantages of auditor involvement in application development. First, the auditor has the opportunity to define his own requirements, which can then be built into the system in the form of an audit subsystem. Through the use of such a subsystem, the auditor can perform a continuous audit of the system. For example, an audit file, containing information on exception conditions, could be reviewed at any time and the authenticity of these items verified.

Second, when a system is only reviewed immediately before its implementation into production, it is more difficult to correct control weaknesses within the system. The following activities should therefore be completed before the auditor reviews a developing application:
- Review the project methodology within the DP department for developing application systems, and report any weaknesses or omissions. This review is necessary because the auditor will subsequently rely on compliance with this methodology as a vehicle for the effective and efficient development of application systems.
- Develop a checklist of the audit department's activities, requirements, and outputs for each of the various stages of development as defined by the methodology.
- Present an audit document to the DP department, and establish a protocol between the two departments to ensure that the audit department is made aware of significant events regarding the development of new applications.
- Establish the criteria for determining which applications will be reviewed during development.

Ongoing Application Audits. In an ongoing application system, the auditor must first identify the location of the controls within the system by documenting the system from a control standpoint. If the auditor was involved in the development of the system, this documentation should be available in the permanent file; otherwise, the auditor must search existing documentation (e.g., data control manual or user manual) to build up control documentation. After the auditor has completed and verified this control documentation, he should be able to judge the overall adequacy of the intended level of control within the system and to plan the extent and type of testing required. The next phase of the audit involves testing the controls within the system and reporting findings and recommendations to management.

The objectives of an ongoing application audit can be generalized as follows:

DEFINING THE SCOPE OF CONTROLS

- The accounting principles incorporated into the application are consistent with generally accepted accounting practices, company policy, and all legal requirements.
- The division of duties among noncompatible functions is adequate.
- The degree of user participation in the design, development, and testing of changes to the application system is adequate.
- All data transmitted and captured by the application system is authorized, complete, and accurate.
- All material calculation routines are correct, and calculated amounts are applied correctly.
- The application system detects and reports all errors and provides an adequate audit trail for all transactions posted or applied.
- The reporting mechanism within the application system provides information that is accurate, complete, timely, and relevant to the user's business needs.
- The contingency plans for prolonged downtime of hardware, software, or telecommunications are adequate.
- All documentation related to the application system is maintained at a level sufficient to facilitate a successful and continued operation.

ADVANCED AUDIT TECHNIQUES

User departments are generally audited annually, while applications are audited less often. In order to provide management with a meaningful report on the adequacy and reliability of the total system, the auditor must have a greater involvement with the computer application and a better understanding of the relationship between the controls within this area of the system and the controls maintained within the user department.

Because of time constraints, however, the auditor must use the computer as an audit tool and implement advanced audit techniques to provide in-depth audit coverage. The following advanced audit techniques can assist the auditor in his evaluation of internal control and system integrity and adequacy.

Regression Testing Facility. A regression testing facility requires setting up test master and transaction files containing all known conditions. Each record is documented, stating its contents and purpose during the running of a test. The documentation for the transaction file should also contain a section on the expected results after application of the transaction. Tests of the system are run using these files. Whenever the system is changed, or at the time of an audit, the tests can be rerun and the two sets of output compared. Any unexpected discrepancies must be followed up by the auditor conducting the test. Output results can be compared manually or by an automated file compare facility.

A regression testing facility requires a high degree of documentation and a commitment to keep both the documentation and the files in line with the current production environment (e.g., when a new condition is encountered in the production environment, the testing files and documentation must be updated to incorporate this new condition).

Integrated Test Facility (ITF). In an ITF, certain test records are incorporated into the live master file. Tests are conducted using these records, which can be amended or deleted; additional records can be created, depending on the requirements of the test. By using the ITF, auditors can submit transactions for processing by the production system without disrupting the run. Care must be taken, however, to ensure that the ITF records are not confused with live data and are not used in reporting actual company results.

Audit Subsystem. As previously stated, an audit subsystem designed into the user system allows the auditor to produce output that can be used in future audits of the system.

Parallel Simulation. Here, the auditor writes a computer program to simulate the functions of the live system that must be tested (e.g., calculation routines or complex logic conditions). The auditor then uses the same input data used to run the live system as input to the simulated system. In this way, the auditor can independently verify the accuracy of the output produced by the live system.

CONCLUSION

The scope of DP controls encompasses the user department and all functions within the DP department. In examining these controls, the auditor must develop an approach that covers all of these areas. This chapter advocates an approach that considers the scope of DP as a single environment with multiple applications running within it.

After assessing the adequacy of control within the environment, the auditor can better determine the level of control necessary within each application system and the extent of audit testing required. In addition, the auditor must become familiar with the interaction between controls in the user department and those in the computer application system if he is to provide a meaningful report on the overall adequacy of control within each application and within the organization.

③ Writing EDP Audit Reports

by William E. Perry

INTRODUCTION

EDP audit reports pose three problems to the auditor. First, the reports usually discuss both the user application and a DP system; thus, most EDP audit reports address two audiences. Second, acronyms and jargon familiar to DP personnel may be unknown to non-DP personnel. Third, few auditors have DP skills sufficient for developing complete recommendations. The auditor therefore must often defend a recommendation while lacking the necessary knowledge to fully support it.

Specific complaints lodged against EDP audit reports include:
- Excessive technical jargon—Because of the DP and in-house jargon present in EDP audit reports, they are nearly incomprehensible to the non-DP professional. EDP audit reports are read by people responsible for acting on report findings and recommendations; their task is more difficult if they cannot understand the intent or impact of those findings and recommendations.
- Generalized findings and recommendations—The report may allude to weak input controls, for example, but not name specific areas of weakness. Such findings are both difficult to comprehend and to correct. The audit report must be specific when identifying areas of weakness in highly complex systems.
- Omission of recommendation side effects—Changes to a data element or system can cause a cascading series of changes in other programs or systems. The actual cost and effort to make a change thus can greatly exceed the apparent cost in the audit report. Frequently, costs exceed benefits.
- Omission of less costly alternatives—Many audit recommendations appear to present "all or nothing" recommendations. When given leeway in solving a problem, DP may find a feasible solution; however, DP may reject a recommendation that contains no options.

These complaints about EDP audit reports highlight the need for EDP auditors to reevaluate report-writing methods and report content. This chapter examines the types of EDP audit reports and proposes recommendations to make them more effective.

TYPES OF EDP AUDIT REPORTS

Auditors must identify the types of reports and the characteristics of each. The common assumption that all audit reports are identical leads to many problems in audit recommendation acceptance.

The five EDP audits performed by auditors are:
- Automated application audits
- Systems development audits
- Post-installation audits
- Computer center audits
- Procedural audits

The type of review conducted affects the style and purpose of the audit report. The review of an operational application is factual, for example, and this audit report is designed to identify, substantiate, and correct weaknesses in the application. The report should be factual and can be direct in presenting the severity of a problem and the need for correction. A systems development audit, however, is one in which the auditor participates with the project team in developing control solutions. This audit report must be carefully couched in team-player terminology to avoid severing the important but fragile lines of communication between the systems analyst and the auditor.

Exit Conference

The exit conference is the proving ground for audit reports. The auditor faces two major risks in issuing an audit report, both of which can be minimized through proper use of the exit conference. The first risk is incorrect data, and the second is the auditee's refusal to accept the recommendations.

At the exit conference prior to issuing the report, the auditor can significantly reduce the probability that these events might occur. First, the auditor should specifically ask the auditee if he or she concurs that the factual information in the report is correct. Second, the auditor can ascertain which recommendations, if any, are unacceptable to the auditee. This provides the auditor two opportunities. Auditor and auditee can compromise on an acceptable solution, or if the auditor feels strongly about a recommendation, he or she can build a case for implementing it prior to issuing the report to senior management. It would be unusual for senior management to reject an audit recommendation accepted by the auditee.

Elements of a Successful EDP Audit Report

Four general guidelines for writing effective EDP audit reports can be applied to every report type. Audit reports should:
- Present explicit findings and recommendations—The auditor should conduct sufficient investigation to ensure that the findings or recommendations are stated clearly enough to guarantee a common understanding between auditor and auditee. The auditor may need to confer

with systems analysts/programmers to accurately describe the intended solution.
- Use supportable findings and recommendations—The auditor must substantiate findings and recommendations with sufficient evidence; unsupported findings and options undermine credibility. Painstaking investigation may be necessary to provide complete assurance of findings and recommendations in highly complex systems; however, this step is usually unnecessary.
- Develop cost-effective solutions—Auditors should recommend control solutions only after the cost-effectiveness of those solutions has been verified. Recommendations that are not cost-effective can be reworked prior to presentation. Many solutions may be found unacceptable because the cost-effectiveness is unknown. These could have been acceptable if the cost of correcting those problems were known and adjustments made accordingly.
- Present acceptable recommendations—Although not every recommendation will be acceptable to the user, the audit group who continually fights with auditees will erode its credibility. Auditors who have done their homework and presold recommendations to auditees, however, will enjoy increased credibility and acceptance of recommendations. Although auditors should not retreat from presenting worthwhile recommendations, they should not insist on the optimal solution if an acceptable solution will be immediately implemented by the auditee.

Report Checklists

Checklists are provided in this chapter for each type of audit report. In addition, there is a general checklist for all types of reports (see Figure 3-1).

The checklist should be used during the early phases of report writing to ensure proper structuring and completeness of the report. The completed checklist should be included with the report.

AUTOMATED APPLICATION AUDIT REPORTS

The automated application audit is the main task of the EDP auditor, who verifies the accuracy, completeness, and authorization of the transactions processed by the application, as well as the controls governing that process.

This audit can involve both the manual and the automated segments of the application. Some organizations limit the EDP audit to the automated segment of the application. Nonetheless, it is usually good practice to audit and report on the integrity of both segments concurrently. Figure 3-2 lists the questions that should be addressed when writing this report.

Report Objectives

The automated application audit report encompasses user activities and the adequacy of the controls in the automated application. The report is thus

Question	Response			Comments
	Yes	No	NA	
Has the report audience been identified?				
Have the findings been reviewed with the auditee to determine accuracy?				
Have the recommendations been reviewed with the auditee to determine agreement with the recommendations? If not, why not?				
Are findings and recommendations explicit enough for the auditee to take action?				
Is there sufficient working paper evidence to support audit findings and recommendations?				
Have report recommendations been evaluated in sufficient detail to determine cost-effectiveness? If recommendations are not cost-effective, do other circumstances warrant including them?				
Will the report be issued on a timely basis so that the maximum benefit can be obtained?				
Does the audit report either eliminate or explain technical DP jargon?				

Figure 3-1. EDP Audit Report General Checklist

Question	Response			Comments
	Yes	No	NA	
If findings are based on information obtained from computer files, does the report indicate whether file integrity has been verified?				
Has the impact of the findings and recommendations been stated in the report?				
Does the auditee agree with the audit finding/recommendation impact as stated?				
Has the impact of the findings and recommendations on other systems been identified and stated?				
If data base technology is used, has the impact of the findings and recommendations on other users of the data base been identified and stated?				
If data base technology is used, has the impact of the findings and recommendations on the data base structure been identified and stated?				

Figure 3-2. Application Audit Report Checklist

directed to the user and the application maintenance team and must clearly identify the personnel responsible for any identified problems.

Because changes to an operational application may cost significantly more than making the same changes to a system under development, the method of installing the change should be addressed in the audit report. Automated application audit reports can be ineffective if too little effort is expended on developing economical solutions to problems.

Report Concerns

In writing the automated application audit report, the auditor must consider:

- Verification of file integrity—When audit findings are based on information contained in computer files, the auditor must substantiate file integrity. If the auditor chooses not to verify the integrity of the file, the audit report should state this. The auditor need not verify a file whose integrity has been proved by another audit; however, he or she should not mislead the reader regarding the integrity of the data on which the audit findings are based.
- Impact of audit findings—The audit report should state the quantitative and qualitative impact of the audit findings on the organization. The auditee or management should not have to decide whether the finding has minimal or significant consequences. The auditor should express this impact in quantitative terms, but if that information proves difficult to obtain or estimate, a qualitative statement is better than ignoring the magnitude of the finding.
- Effect on other applications—The auditor must investigate the possible effects of findings and recommendations on other application systems. For example, a recommendation that adds control information to a record can affect all other applications that use that record.
- Multi-user systems—If two divisions or departments use the same application system, findings or recommendations may need to be addressed to all application users. Recommendations may be accepted through consensus by the user who bears primary responsibility for the application.
- Data base considerations—Both current and future impact of audit findings must be assessed in a data base environment. The use and control of the data base must be optimized for the entire organization—not just a single application. In addition, future applications must interface with the data base. Recommended application changes that affect the data base must be reviewed with the data base administrator. Recommendations resulting from a data base audit, however, must be viewed from the perspective of every application using that data.

SYSTEMS DEVELOPMENT AUDIT REPORTS

Audit participation in systems development is one of the best uses of internal audit time because controls not installed during systems development may not be economical to install later. The purpose of systems development audit reports is predictive. The auditor estimates the adequacy of controls in the future, based on the adequacy of proposed or partially developed controls at the time of the audit. Figure 3-3 provides a checklist for writing a systems development audit report.

Question	Response Yes	Response No	Response NA	Comments
Has the source of the findings and recommendations been identified if other than the auditor?				
Is the report issued on a timely basis to ensure the most economical installation of recommendations?				
Has the individual responsible for control recommendations been identified?				
Will the controls, standards, and guidelines recommended during the review be applicable when the system is placed into production?				
Will there be standards, regulations, guidelines, or controls needed at the time the system goes into operation that are not needed now?				
Has management been informed of the reliability of the audit opinion?				
Have technological controls been separated from application controls in the report findings and recommendations?				
Has the adequacy of needed techological controls been assessed by an auditor with the necessary technical skills?				

Figure 3-3. Systems Development Audit Report Checklist

Report Objectives

The systems development audit report is written primarily for the systems development project team to provide them with an assessment of the controls being developed for the application. The report usually does not recommend additional controls but instead identifies areas of weakness, leaving the development of solutions to the project team. (Auditors who recommend control solutions may have difficulty objectively assessing the controls they recommend.)

Systems development audit reports should be issued immediately upon the conclusion of the review. The earlier in the development cycle that recommendations are made, the more economical and easier the solution.

Report Concerns

In writing the systems development audit report, the auditor should consider the following:

- Source of recommendations—Systems development is a creative process in which individuals from different backgrounds and disciplines contribute to solving a business problem. The auditor frequently participates in this free and open development process, out of which he or she must create a report that often includes recommendations that have been discussed with the project team. If the auditor appears to take credit for what the project team believes is a group-generated solution, idea-generating sessions will no longer occur when the auditor is present. The auditor should ensure that the reports give appropriate credit to the project team for team-generated solutions.
- Personnel responsible for control—Since control development procedures are new to most organizations, controls often are neither well understood nor fully developed. Audit recommendations should specifically name those responsible for indicated control actions.
- Reliability of audit opinion—Most audit reports are based on historical data and thus exhibit a high degree of reliability; a systems development audit, however, presents a predictive opinion. Management should not be misled into thinking that the prediction of future events contained in the systems development audit report carries the same reliability as opinions based on historic events.
- Technological controls—Application system needs can be implemented through operating software. Since the controls within the operating software, and those between the application system and the operating software, can be technically complex, special skills may be needed to assess them and to properly identify control weaknesses.

POST-INSTALLATION AUDIT REPORTS

The post-installation audit is designed to verify compliance of the application with user specifications. This one-time audit occurs shortly after the system becomes operational. Figure 3-4 shows a post-installation audit report checklist.

Report Objectives

The post-installation audit report is designed to give users and management an assessment of the operational system's compliance with specifications and to identify areas of noncompliance. Although other problems may be reported, the report should concentrate on noncompliance with systems specifications.

Report Concerns

In writing the post-installation audit report, the auditor should consider:
- Applicability of system specifications—Because systems development takes months or years, specifications determined during needs analysis may no longer be applicable. Reasons for this include changing busi-

Question	Response			Comments
	Yes	No	NA	
Has user desire for the implementation of the defined system specifications been determined?				
Was DP provided the correct system specifications?				
Does the scope of the audit report clearly state the objectives of the post-installation audit?				
Does the report indicate the percentage of noncompliance items in the total system?				
Was sufficient shakedown time allowed before performing the post-installation audit?				
Does the report clearly state that the user desires to have implemented specifications that were not included in the operational system?				

Figure 3-4. Post-Installation Audit Report Checklist

ness conditions, new user management, or the development of a better solution to the problem.

- User requirements—Prior to conducting the audit, the auditor must confirm user requirements with the users themselves. It serves no purpose to verify noncompliance with specifications the user no longer desires.
- Application shakedown—New application systems can be expected to encounter problems during the early stages of operation. One problem may be noncompliance with system specifications. The application team should be given reasonable time to shake down the new system and to make necessary corrections.

COMPUTER CENTER AUDIT REPORTS

The computer center is responsible for operating the application. The computer center may not be a single room but a network of facilities held together by a communications system. In addition, the computer center usually has responsibility for data security.

To fulfill computer center responsibilities, several functions must be established. These include data libraries, production scheduling and control, and job accounting. The audit can include any or all of these activities. Figure 3-5 lists questions to be answered when writing a computer center audit report.

Report Objectives

The computer center audit report reviews compliance with and effectiveness of the general controls governing computer operations. Report topics

WRITING AUDIT REPORTS

Question	Response			Comments
	Yes	No	NA	
Does the audit report state the scope of the audit?				
Does the audit report indicate the auditor's qualifications to perform the audit?				
Does the audit report indicate which major controls in the computer center have not been tested?				
If significant activities are not audited, does the report clearly state that these activities have been omitted from the audit?				
Are vendor products that contain control weaknesses identified?				
Are the parties responsible for correcting the vendor problems identified?				
Are all involved parties aware of computer center control weaknesses?				

Figure 3-5. Computer Center Audit Report Checklist

range from such nontechnical matters as the accuracy of user chargebacks to such technical subjects as controls over the program library.

Report Concerns

In writing the computer center audit report, the auditor should consider:
- Audit scope—The auditor should clearly state the computer center activities covered by the report.
- Auditor qualifications—The audit report should state the auditor's qualifications to perform the computer center audit. If highly technical areas are reviewed, auditor competence in these areas should be stated. This background information assists management in evaluating the reliability of audit findings and recommendations. It also enables the auditors to limit the scope of the audit based upon the experiences of the audit team.
- Controls function—Many controls in the computer center are designed to prevent or to recover from serious problems. For example, disaster planning involves developing the procedures and acquiring the tools necessary to recover from a major problem. Such plans may never be tested if the disaster does not occur. The audit report should indicate whether these controls have been tested, since untested controls may not work when needed.
- Vendor problems—If there are control deficiencies in vendor hardware or software, the vendor should be identified in the audit report. Bringing the group responsible for correcting the deficiency to management's attention facilitates correction. It also relieves computer center management of possible blame for vendor problems.

PROCEDURAL AUDIT REPORTS

Systems and programming personnel implement procedures for development and maintenance activities. These procedures are usually a combination of standards and guidelines to ensure uniformity of systems development and ease of systems maintenance. Figure 3-6 provides a checklist for writing procedural audit reports.

Question	Response			Comments
	Yes	No	NA	
Has the originator of the deficient procedure been identified?				
Are the procedural recommendations written in a manner to encourage management support?				
Has the impact of the new procedure been stated?				
Does the new procedure require that existing applications be modified?				
Has the cost of compliance for both old and new systems been identified?				
Has the impact of one procedural deficiency on other procedures been evaluated?				
Have all systems and activities affected by the procedural recommendation been identified?				
Has the method of ensuring compliance with the new procedure been identified?				

Figure 3-6. Procedural Review Audit Report Checklist

Report Objectives

The objective of the procedural audit report is to assess systems development standards and guidelines. Weaknesses in these procedures result in ineffective, uneconomical, or poorly controlled application systems. The report is directed to DP management and identifies general control weaknesses for DP management to correct.

Procedural audits, in effect, evaluate DP management; therefore, the audit is usually done by senior EDP auditors knowledgeable in both systems development and in the organization's policies and procedures.

Report Concerns

In writing the procedural audit report, the auditor should consider:
- Management involvement in procedure development—Procedures may have been developed or introduced by the manager receiving the audit

report. Stating recommendations diplomatically thus may be necessary to gain their acceptance. This concern is a reality of the business world; however, the auditor must not mislead management by writing unclear reports.
- Procedural finding/recommendation impact—Many procedures are based on opinion and, without sufficient analysis, may remain unsubstantiated. Auditors should state the quantitative or qualitative impact if the recommendation is not adopted.
- Effect on old systems—If a procedure is to be changed, it must be determined whether existing applications must be modified to ensure compliance with the new procedure.

CONCLUSION

Effective EDP audit reports help ensure the implementation of audit recommendations. In order to maximize audit effectiveness and minimize report-writing costs, EDP audit report-writing guidelines should be issued. These guidelines should provide a plan of action for improving EDP audit reports and should include:
- Identifying the report type prior to writing the report
- Developing the report to address the report-writing concerns
- Using a report-writing checklist to measure the adequacy and completeness of the report

These measures will assist in producing audit reports that state findings clearly and that are acceptable to management.

# 4 Auditing DP Standards

by Ben G. Matley
and David W. Syfritt

INTRODUCTION

The place of the DP standards audit within the EDP audit is the first of four problems addressed in this chapter, followed by:
- DP standards to be audited
- The audit process
- Special considerations concerning how organization size and industry DP practices affect DP standards

A brief checklist regarding DP standards and points for discussion between the organization and its general auditor to be resolved prior to the next general audit are also presented.

THE PLACE OF THE DP STANDARDS AUDIT

DP standards, like all work standards, are part of the management control function. Because they are part of DP, they are audited during the EDP audit.

The American Institute of Certified Public Accountants (AICPA) *Statement on Auditing Standards* (SAS-3), AU Section 321, paragraph 03, includes the EDP audit in the general accounting audit:

> A data processing system may be wholly manual or may include a combination of manual activities, mechanical activities, and electronic data processing activities (EDP) . . . In some data processing systems, accounting control procedures are performed by people in one or more departments. In EDP systems, many or even most of these control procedures may be performed by the EDP process itself. When EDP is used in significant accounting applications, the auditor should consider the EDP activity in his study and evaluation of accounting controls.

Acting on this recommendation, the California CPA Foundation for Education and Research (Cal-CPA) developed an approach to the EDP audit that divides DP accounting controls into two classifications: general and applications controls.

General DP controls affect all DP applications and, therefore, all DP accounting applications. Application controls affect only a single DP accounting program. Such payroll program controls as cross-footing totals, for example, ensure that the sum of all withholdings plus the sum of net pays balances with the sum of gross pays; this control affects only payroll accounting. On the other hand, DP programming (work) and documentation standards affect all DP applications; therefore, DP standards fit within the category of general accounting controls.

DP STANDARDS TO BE AUDITED

The classification of DP standards depends on the organization. Large software shops might have a separate software quality control or DP standards group that develops a formal DP standards manual. This group may also perform internal EDP audits in some organizations (e.g., internal accounting audits, quality assurance audits, and management audits). Medium or small organizations, however, may rely on simple lists of guidelines prepared by the DP manager or other senior staff members. General agreement about several specifics on those lists can be expected, whether the lists are prepared by DP, accounting, or specialized EDP audit personnel.

This section contains an abbreviated list of DP standards as DP personnel perceive them and then reorganizes the list to parallel more closely the SAS-3 statements and terminology.

DP's List of DP Standards

It is common for DP personnel to think in terms of general categories (e.g., programming, data entry, operations or hardware, software, data, and personnel). DP personnel thus think of standards as they apply to each category. For the sake of example, the categories software standards, data standards, and documentation standards are used here. Specifics include:
- Software standards
  —Design standards. The steps in the design process; the forms for software requests, approvals, and structured design specifications; points for design review.
  —Applications standards. The controls common to all application programs, the specific controls for certain applications.
  —Coding standards. Writing style and sentence structure (e.g., indentation, nesting restrictions, self-explanatory error messages).
  —Testing standards. Who tests, when, and how; use of test data generators; delivery of test results and documents; independent quality-control testing.
  —Release and change control standards. The steps in those procedures; forms for transfer to production; reporting of production problems; program change request, approval, and retest forms.
- Data standards
  —Data naming standards. Those assigned, denied, or optional to the programmer; structure of file qualification names; internal program input, output, and working storage variables.

AUDITING DP STANDARDS

  —File standards. Mandated, denied, or optional file media; file organization methods, formats, and labels; and file retention criteria.
  —Report standards. Those reports intended for human readability; content of headings, body, and footing; forms alignment pages.
  —Library standards. Those at the internal machine level; location and backup procedures; access and password requirements.
- Documentation standards
  —Contents of the documentation library. What is required; who is responsible for each item; checkout procedures.
  —Events to be documented. Those mandated, excluded, or optional; how and by whom; timing requirements.
  —Forms and formats. The standard forms; required or optional information, manner of delivery, and chronological relationship to events.
  —Retention criteria. Mandated and optional holding periods; update criteria.

This list of DP standards as perceived by DP personnel may be quite compatible with a list of DP standards as perceived by accounting personnel and, in particular, as perceived by the General Auditor (GA). The GA, however, will probably express those standards in terminology compatible with the AICPA SAS-3 statement.

GA's List of DP Standards

As previously mentioned, the GA perceives the audit in terms of general and application controls. Following the terminology of the AICPA and Cal-CPA, general accounting controls include seven categories, each of which affect all individual DP applications (i.e., all accounting). The seven categories of general DP controls follow:
- Organization—the human chain of command, DP job specifications, and duties. DP standards are represented either as a standards group in a large organization or as a DP senior staff responsibility in a smaller firm.
- DP operations—controls on machine-room access, specifications for run logs, requirements for operator manuals.
- Documentation—a list of required documentation, retention criteria, access restrictions.
- Systems and program development—the forms and procedures for new software requests and approvals sequences in software design, design review points, acceptance testing, software change control procedures.
- Hardware and systems software—machine-error detection and correction facilities, restrictions on access to the internals, maintenance of systems software and hardware.
- Access and library—controls on access to machine libraries; file naming, labeling, and protection criteria; access logs for physical media; systems logs on file access.
- Judgmental factors—any additional items that the auditor judges perti-

nent to the particular audit setting; for example, ability to continue a critical DP operation despite adverse circumstances (e.g., loss of neighborhood-area power), security of computer-stored assets, backup procedures for both on- and off-site.

The list of DP standards as seen by DP personnel can be merged with the seven categories of GA general controls. For example, all software standards items from the first list fall under the GA category for systems and programs development (with the exception of those items that refer to software internals.) Those excepted items, of course, fall under the hardware and systems software category on the GA list.

The four DP standards in the data standards list would be divided among the seven GA categories as follows:
- Data naming standards—systems and program development
- File standards—access and libraries
- Report standards—systems and program development and/or documentation
- Library standards—access and libraries and/or judgmental factors

Finally, DP standards in the documentation standards list fall entirely under the documentation category on the GA list.

The combined lists provide the specific DP standards to be audited during the EDP audit—in short, all specifics deemed pertinent by both DP and accounting. These specifics can be merged within the seven categories of general accounting controls. Furthermore, concern about pure classifications of specific standards and redundancy is unnecessary. Routine backup instructions may be classified as DP operations, with backup DP centers (for emergency use) listed under "Organization," or all backup considerations may be listed under "DP operations."

Once the specifics to be audited have been identified and arranged under the seven GA categories of general controls, the audit process is implemented.

THE AUDIT PROCESS

The audit process consists of four steps (see Figure 4-1): initial on-site visit, preliminary review, detail review, and substantive testing. Each step has a specific purpose, and the results of the first three steps determine whether the audit process continues or terminates.

Initial On-Site Visit

The purpose of the initial on-site visit is to determine significant accounting applications (those that could materially affect the financial statements of the firm). This is decided through use of a questionnaire that is issued to the controller, DP manager, or other knowledgeable person designated by the client firm.

AUDITING DP STANDARDS

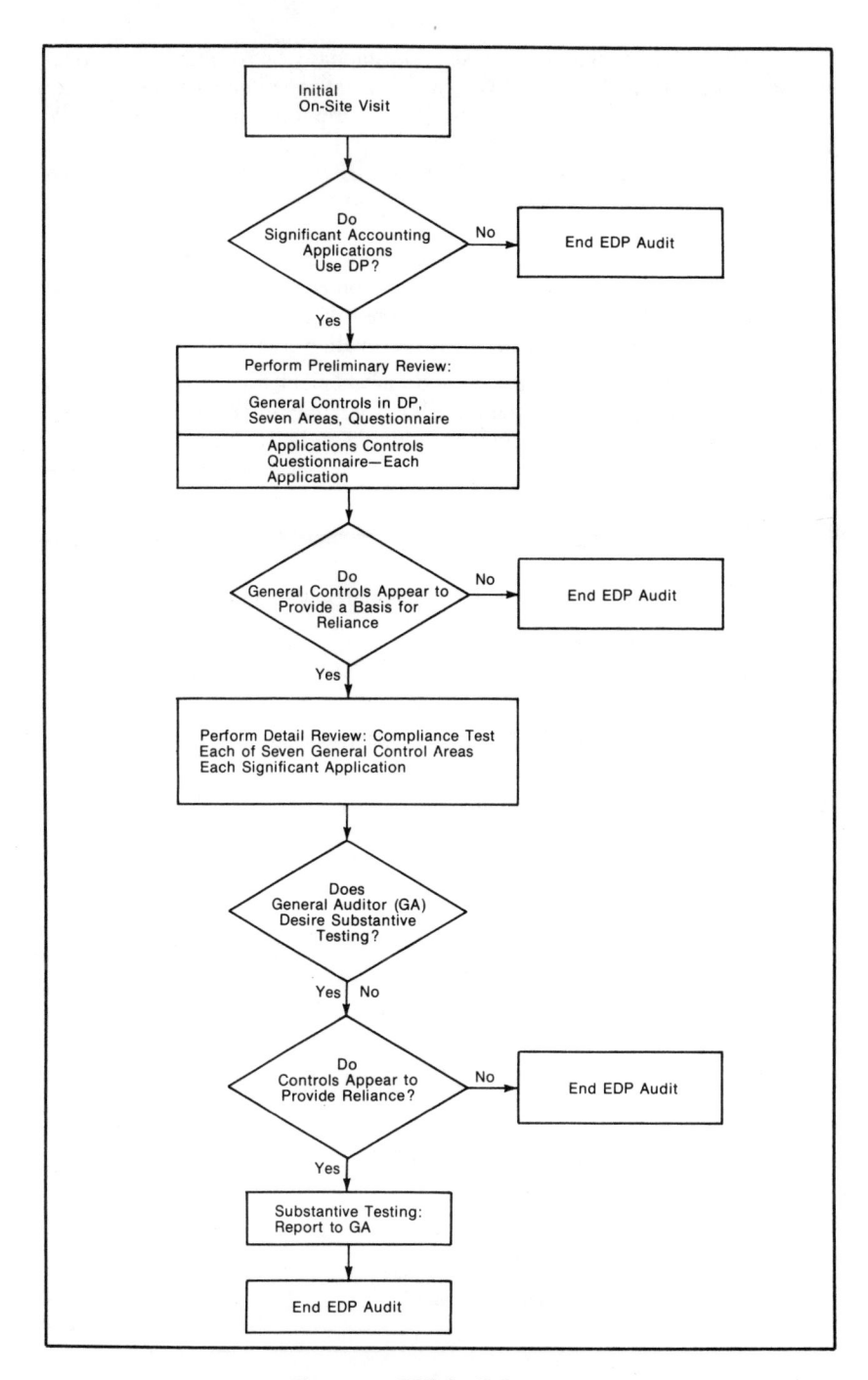

Figure 4-1. EDP Audit Process

The scope of the initial on-site visit is substantially one of inquiry; personal verification by the auditor is not yet involved. Information is gathered on the organization, personnel assignments, job descriptions, major uses of DP, number of DP sites, and the hardware and software configurations at each site. From this information, the GA and the EDP auditor determine which significant accounting applications use DP methods.

Initial On-Site Visit Forms. Examples of the initial on-site visit questionnaire are shown in Figure 4-2. The key question concerns representation and enforcement of DP standards and is answered through determination of the number of audit personnel in the software quality control area.

The DP standards representation and enforcement functions can exist in separate DP standards and internal EDP audit departments in very large organizations or as a single position within DP in smaller organizations.

Initial On-Site Visit Questionnaire

General Information—EDP

1. Name of EDP auditor asking these questions and completing this form:
   _____ Date _____
2. Name of CPA client firm _____
3. Name of (subject) firm audited _____
4. Name and title _____
   _____
5. Name and title of person who is the primary respondent to these questions, if different than No. 4 above: _____
   _____
6. Summary of EDP organization and installation:
   a. DP department is under _____
      (Attach organizational chart or illustrate on back.)
   b. How funded: _____ Departmental budget _____ Bill users _____
   c. Personnel: Total of _____ persons at _____ sites
   d. Data Entry (DE):   ____ Centralized in DP   _____ Distributed
                          ____ Programmable   _____ Interactive DE
                               batch DE
                          ____
   e. Programming: ____ Centralized in DP _____ User & DP departments
                          _____ Batch_____ RJE _____ Interactive
                               local
                          Languages, primary first: _____
   f. Processing: No. of sites with CPUs: _____
                    No. of sites with remote I/O: _____
   g. Output: _____ Local line printer   _____ Remote inquiry
                    _____
      _____ Control of output by DP _____ By others _____
   h. Has a prior EDP audit been performed?
             _____ Yes _____ No   _____ Date
         Is a copy of that final report available? _____

Figure 4-2. Initial On-Site Visit Questionnaire

AUDITING DP STANDARDS

7. Personnel—Enter number of persons in each EDP activity area, by level:

	Data Entry	Data Control	Systems & Programming	Operating Schedule	Software QC EDP Audit DP Standards
Managers/ Supervisors					
Audit/Quality Control					
Systems Analysis					
Programming					
CPU Operations					
Terminal Operators					
Data Entry Operations					
Data Control/ Control Clerk					
Librarian					
Typists/Clerks/ Receptionists					
DP Standards Supervisor					
Other (list)					

Figure 4-2 (Cont)

Where no formal DP standards are claimed, the general accounting audit of DP standards stops (although DP may be audited for the other reasons discussed later in this chapter).

The outcome of this step is to determine either that significant accounting applications do not use DP methods (the audit terminates) or that these applications do use DP methods (and the audit proceeds to the next step, preliminary review of DP standards).

Preliminary Review

The purpose of the preliminary review is to assess whether there appears to be a basis for reliance on DP controls, including DP standards, as part of accounting control. The auditor must first determine which DP standards exist and the degree to which they are implemented.

Information is obtained from questionnaires—one for each category of general DP controls previously discussed. In addition, a set of application questionnaires is developed for each significant accounting application identified during the initial on-site visit.

Since the preliminary review begins with questionnaire information, it is vital that a knowledgeable senior person be the respondent. During the preliminary review, the auditor may have the opportunity for personal observation and confirmation of responses, while still depending primarily on questionnaire information.

The information gathered during this step is divided into three classes—input, processing, and output. Each significant accounting application reflects DP standards because it involves an application program. Investigation, therefore, should focus on the inclusion of specific DP standards in individual programs. The preliminary review is general in scope; for example, the auditor should not read the payroll program to assess its compliance with standards but should instead ascertain which standards the client is attempting to implement.

Preliminary Review Forms. The forms used in the preliminary review step should be organized under the seven categories of GA controls listed previously. Samples from two categories (organization and DP operations) are provided in Figures 4-3 and 4-4. The forms are checkoff questionnaires. The next-to-last column at the right of the form, labeled "Source of Information (C, A, or CA)," as suggested by the Cal-CPA, should be answered by the client alone (C), the auditor (A), or the client with confirmation from the auditor (CA).

Assessing Controls in Organization	Appropriate to this type and size installation?			Contributes to possible reliance?		Source of Information	Comment
	Yes	Possibly	No	Yes	No	(C, A, or CA)	
Can DP personnel authorize financial transactions? Who? Which?							
Can DP personnel authorize DP transactions? Who? Which?							
Manner and degree of supervision of DP personnel?							
Are there formal DP standards?							

Preliminary Review Questionnaire
General Controls
Page _____ of _____

Comments:
Apparent reliance in this area? Yes _____ No _____
Generally accepted DP practices for this size center? Yes _____ No _____

CPA client _____ Firm audited _____ Date _____ Initial _____

Figure 4-3. Preliminary Review Questionnaire: General Controls (Organization)

AUDITING DP STANDARDS

Assessing Controls in DP Operations	Appropriate to this type and size installation? Yes	Possibly	No	Contributes to possible reliance? Yes	No	Source of Information (C, A, or CA)	Comment
Preliminary Review Questionnaire — General Controls — Name of person answering questionnaire _____ Page ___ of ___							
Are computer transactions periodically reviewed? How? By whom?							
How are computer activities supervised?							
DP personnel precluded from initiating or authorizing transactions?							
Operating personnel restricted from access to systems and program documentation?							
Is run log kept?							
Does log record each operator intervention?							
Operator instruction manual? Adequate exception procedures?							
Is physical access to computer, data entry, disk packs, documentation, etc. restricted?							

Comments:
Apparent reliance in this area? Yes _____ No _____
Generally accepted DP practices for this size center? Yes _____ No _____

CPA client _____ Firm audited _____ Date _____ Initial _____

Figure 4-4. Preliminary Review Questionnaire: General Controls (DP Operations)

Since DP standards are part of general controls, they should be reflected in each application. The application control questionnaire (Figure 4-5) should thus include items about DP standards and be divided into input, processing, and output sections. (A sample questionnaire for assessing controls in input is provided in Figure 4-5.) Because DP standards within applications control affect all applications, the questionnaire should be replicated for each application. Individual application audit forms will also aid in the detail review step.

The outcome of the preliminary review is either:
- The items on the list of DP standards are said to be represented completely, partially, or not at all within the seven categories of DP general controls.

- The program and DP procedures for each significant accounting application are said to have been developed completely, partially, or not at all with respect to existing DP standards.

If general DP controls (including DP standards) and individual application controls appear to provide a basis for reliance, the audit proceeds to the detail review step.

Detail Review

The detail review provides visual verification that DP standards are being adhered to. The AICPA SAS-3 refers to tests for compliance where the preliminary review has indicated an apparent basis of reliance on DP general controls. The purpose of the detail review is to obtain some verification that the controls stated to exist are in fact evident. Such evidence is obtained from the EDP auditor's observation of DP activities and examination of documentation written after those DP standards have been implemented.

Name of person answering questionnaire _____	Preliminary Review Questionnaire Application Controls for the _____ Application Page ____ of ____						
Assessing Controls in Input	Appropriate to this type and size installation?			Contributes to possible reliance?		Source of Information	Comment
	Yes	Possibly	No	Yes	No	(C, A, or CA)	
Is input approved by signature of an authorized person?							
Is input request submitted on a standard form?							
Are prenumbered transmittal forms used?							
Are source documents on standard prenumbered forms?							
Are small batches used?							
Are batch/hash totals used?							
Are record counts made?							
Are source documents and transmittal forms cancelled?							

Comments:
Apparent reliance in this area? Yes _____ No _____
Generally accepted DP practices for this size center? Yes _____ No _____

CPA client _____ Firm audited _____ Date _____ Initial _____

Figure 4-5. Preliminary Review Questionnaire: Application Controls (Input)

AUDITING DP STANDARDS

There is a limitation on the scope of inquiry in the detail review, namely, that limited observations of a complex and continuous process are made for brief periods only. Although a formal DP standards manual and the documentation on program testing and release can be seen, for example, it can only be assumed that those documents were in fact generated during the program design process and not later. A fair perspective must be maintained concerning the scope of the detail review; it is limited to the observation of evidence of compliance with the stated DP standards.

Detail review should begin with the DP standards listed previously (the seven categories of DP general controls). Evidence of compliance with each specific DP standard should be gathered. Such evidence includes observation of actual work sequences and examination of documentation. The auditor should observe who is in the DP center, that the operator did or did not have access to the program documents, that the operator did log in and out the tapes and disks used, and that the programmer was writing in the indented style for writing code. In addition to observing work activities, the auditor can examine the materials in the documentation library.

Detail Review Forms. Since the detail review involves visual verification, the preliminary review questionnaires can be used. There is room on the form for a dual entry for each item should the "C" and "A" responses differ. When each response can be reported as "A" and "C," the detail review is complete. This step requires hours of research, observation, and documentation study.

Having observed and recorded the evidence of compliance with DP standards, the auditor must determine whether the evidence still indicates reliance on general DP controls. The GA makes the final decision concerning whether the DP standards observed provide sufficient reliance. If the GA desires further proof of reliance, the EDP audit continues to the last step, substantive testing.

Substantive Testing

Unlike the first three steps in the audit process, substantive testing does not depend on questionnaire responses. The auditor discovers through personal investigation. The software itself is used to examine the internal content of the program. For example, utility programs can extract random samples of data records and program segments that are compared with known standards to detect variances.

In addition to using the installation's own software, the EDP auditor may also employ unique auditing programs. The EDP auditor should design unique test data for processing by individual application programs to determine that the programs were indeed designed with respect to the specified program standards. The substantive testing step of the audit thus becomes a separate and technical study.

ADDITIONAL CONSIDERATIONS IN AUDITING DP STANDARDS

The process of auditing DP standards and the sample forms presented here can only be adapted to a particular organization after several additional factors are considered. These factors include:
- Security concerns, which arise as outside persons penetrate the DP environment
- Service center processing, which introduces a third party to the audit
- Additional reasons for auditing DP, which may extend beyond the traditional general accounting audit and may introduce new views of the EDP audit
- Organization size and industry practice, which might preclude certain desired practices because of economic limitations

Security. The auditor, like all outside consultants, represents a security risk. The auditor is given access to more of the system than are most of the firm's own employees, especially when substantive testing takes place. No firm should refuse to be audited for this reason, but acknowledgment of the risk should lead to greater care in audit design.

Data security is also threatened when both teleprocessing and data base methods are in use. Most business data is transmitted over nonsecure telephone systems and is rarely encrypted. In these circumstances, a highly secure central site becomes vulnerable through its communications network.

Service Center Processing. Service centers, and other forms of shared off-site processors, lead to the introduction of independent third parties into the audit process. Such centers have their own security and general DP standards on which all users depend. Any given user who is audited, therefore, is dependent on the center's auditor for enforcement of DP standards.

Additional Reasons for Auditing DP Standards. The first reason for performing substantive testing is to determine the extent to which inadequate DP standards might damage or circumvent traditional accounting controls found in other departments. In the absence of proper DP standards, each programmer and analyst is free to design applications in any manner desired. Since the computer can thoroughly undo conventional accounting controls found in other departments, however, the absence of DP controls (in particular, DP standards) can place the organization in double jeopardy—no DP contribution to reliance on controls and negation of reliable, traditional non-DP controls.

The AICPA Commission on Auditors' Responsibilities suggested in its *Report of Tentative Conclusions* two additional reasons for auditing DP: fraud (and the necessity to audit specifically for such in DP systems) and year-round DP auditing.

The concern for fraud can be addressed by an audit to test where DP might circumvent traditional controls. That situation certainly offers the potential for fraud, and much fraud has been enabled by a lack of DP standards.

AUDITING DP STANDARDS

Table 4-1. DP Standards: Immediate Audit Concerns

	Yes/No Response		Not Applicable	Need to Implement	Needs Improvement	Satisfactory
	by DP Manager	by Controller				
1. Does the organization chart show a DP standards department or subdepartment?						
2. Are there formal, published DP standards in: a. Systems? b. Documentation? c. Application programs? d. Operations? e. Access & library?						
3. If No. 1 is no: a. Are there any positions with job descriptions that include preparing DP standards? b. If not, should there not be at least one?						
4. Is there an internal EDP audit department or subdepartment?						
5. If No. 4 is no: a. Are there any positions that call for audit of DP standards internally? b. If not, should there be at least one person to do random samples, part time?						
6. Dollar value annual DP budget _____						
7. Dollar value DP controls _____						

The possible year-round continuous audit of DP standards can be one response to the limitations previously identified in present audits (e.g., the momentary audit of a continuous DP process). An internal EDP audit department can aid in establishing such a continuous audit, to the extent that the GA assists in the audit design and accepts the results.

Organization Size and Industry Practice. As mentioned, large organizations may have funding to support separate DP standards and EDP audit departments. Medium-sized organizations may not; small organizations do not. Large organizations also have sufficient personnel to avoid incompatible assignments, to rotate assignments, and to demand that vacations be taken. Smaller organizations will find these difficult or impossible to achieve. Something can always be achieved in the area of standards, however.

CONCLUSION

DP systems' capabilities have been consistently ahead of applications, and applications have been ahead of controls. DP standards and EDP audit depart-

Table 4-2. Checklist of Matters to Discuss with the GA prior to the Next EDP Audit

1. How does the annual DP budget compare with that of other organizations of this size in this industry?
2. Given the annual DP budget, how does the annual dollar value for DP controls compare with it (include all expenses for standards personnel, internal EDP audit personnel, security, etc.)?
3. What percentage of the accounting budget is allocated to control activities? How does that compare with question 2?
4. What proportion of assets and transactions is stored in the DP system?
5. What percentage of those values would be reasonably invested in controls (i.e., DP standards and internal EDP auditing)?
6. If there is an internal DP standards department and/or internal EDP audit department, should the GA assist in a review of those functions now, prior to the next general audit?
7. Should unannounced, random substantive testing of DP standards and data records be instituted as a defense against fraud?
8. Given the results of the most recent EDP audit, is it possible that inadequate or unreliable DP standards and controls may negate the otherwise effective traditional accounting controls?
9. To what degree might a DP emergency affect DP's ability to operate during and after the emergency?
10. Other?

---

ments likewise lag behind the production processes they purport to control. In addition, auditors should inquire beyond mere questionnaires. The Bar Chris case of the mid-1960s held auditors legally responsible for making legitimate inquiries into an organization, beyond simple questioning of the corporate board.

Although this chapter does not cover every concern about the DP standards audit, brief checklists of general concerns, provided in Tables 4-1 and 4-2, address the auditor's basic concerns about DP standards. Table 4-1 lists immediate concerns and can be answered by both the controller and the DP manager. This approach is in keeping with the view of what is to be audited, namely, all those items deemed necessary by both accounting and DP personnel. Table 4-2 lists matters that must be resolved with the general auditor before the next audit.

5 Test Design for Systems under Development

by Jack B. Mullen

SYSTEM DEVELOPMENT CONTROLS

Various methods are used to implement computer systems—in-house design, turnkey software packages, or a combination thereof. Project administration activities should be consistent for each project. The installation should have documented guidelines standardizing the events in each phase of development. These guidelines, in turn, provide each project leader with a standard reporting contention for each development phase. Thus, the manager of several projects can more easily evaluate the performance of the project leaders by concentrating on the progress of major events.

Each phase, from proposal to implementation, requires that specific facts be gathered and built on as each step gives way to the next logical activity. System development controls ensure that these facts are gathered and documented.

System development guidelines should cover the administrative tasks that must be performed, including:
- Defining the job
- Organizing and staffing
- Time and cost estimating
- Breaking down and assigning job steps
- Procedures for implementing necessary changes
- Criteria for acceptance
- Minimum standards for communication

The system development control review requires a great deal of auditor judgment to ascertain how, when, and why to react to apparent problems. The timing of reporting exceptions is highly critical because the circumstances of an exception could change quickly. The auditor must immediately research the problem and bring it to the attention of management. Less time is required to correct problems early in the system development life cycle than is required during a later phase.

Test Design Checklist

The development process should be planned and organized to progress in phases with appropriate checkpoints for management review and sign-off.

Control Objective. To ensure the justification proposal contains sufficient relevant information, is supported by adequate research, is formulated with adequate participation from all appropriate personnel, and proves the cost-effectiveness of continuing the project to the feasibility phase.

Audit Objective. To determine whether the justification proposal is accurate and contains all relevant data.

Audit Test. The justification proposal should be evaluated as follows:
- The scope and purpose of the system should be completely defined.
- User requirements should be generally defined.
- Desired improvements and the benefits resulting from the new system should be explained and supported by adequate evidence.
- All reasonable alternatives should be explained in terms that easily show the most cost-effective approach.
- Costs and benefits should be accurately calculated and presented in a comparative analysis.
- A reasonable estimate of the time required to develop the proposed system should be disclosed.
- All existing and anticipated development problems should be disclosed.
- Project and system objectives should be clearly defined.
- Through interviews, the auditor should determine that all concerned parties participated in preparation of the proposal.
- The auditor determines, to the extent possible, whether the proposed system reduces control in a particular area.

Control Objective. To ensure that an adequate investigation is conducted to prove the feasibility of the proposed system development.

Audit Objective. To determine whether the content of the feasibility study is accurate.

Audit Test. This test determines that the study's approach was logically developed and that the problem was factually presented through an in-depth review of the feasibility documentation:
- I/O requirements should be clearly defined.
- System flows should be clearly and logically presented.
- Anticipated costs and benefits for all alternatives should be reasonably supported and comparatively presented.
- All existing and anticipated project problems should be accurately disclosed and solutions recommended.
- All interdependencies of this project schedule with other project schedules should be described.
- An overview of the study, adequately summarizing its aspects, should be included.
- A preliminary implementation plan should be prepared. This plan should outline the start and target dates as well as estimated hours for each of the following phases:

TEST DESIGN FOR SYSTEMS UNDER DEVELOPMENT

  —User requirement preparation
  —Package evaluation or design specification
  —Functional or package modification specifications
  —Programming
  —Testing
- This plan should also outline:
  —The expectations of the project
  —Major events
  —Manpower estimates
- The feasibility study should address the problems implied by the goals and objectives cited in the proposal.
- The study should be thorough in its scope of investigation.
- The estimated schedule, costs, and personnel requirements should be conservative but realistic.
- The auditor must judge if the final recommendations of the study are accurate and based on solid facts.
- The proposed system should meet the needs of the user.
- The auditor must judge the feasibility of the design schedule.
- The proposed software and hardware must be sufficient to handle the processing of the new system.

Control Objective. To adequately isolate and document the user requirements that will provide a basis for the design or package evaluation.

Audit Objective. To determine whether the user requirements contain everything necessary for system processing and control.

Audit Tests. The user requirements should be evaluated to ascertain that they were prepared in detail and with the user's participation:
- The user requirements should be sufficiently detailed to serve as the primary package selection or design criteria.
- The information required on computer reports should be presented in a detailed, accurate, and useful form.
- The specifications should describe how input will be controlled and reflected on computer reports.
- All applicable legal requirements should be satisfied by the system.
- Three system controls should be defined as necessary:
  —Input and source document control
  —Programmatic edits
  —Output and balancing controls
- Error correction procedures should be defined.
- A conversion plan should be properly defined.
- All necessary documentation should be completed and should comply with in-house guidelines.
- Proposed system processing should satisfy the needs of the user.
- The user should completely review the requirements, sign off, and formally approve continuation.

Control Objective. To provide a general design of the proposed system.

Audit Objective. To determine whether the general design was prepared from the user requirements, satisfies the needs cited in the proposal, and addresses the elements of the feasibility study.

Audit Test. The general design should be reviewed for completeness, and it should be determined that the design does not intend to automate the inefficiencies of a current system or procedure:
- The design should satisfy the requirements cited in the proposal and feasibility study as well as those cited by the user.
- Input and output requirements should be defined and documented.
- Structural definitions of all anticipated files should be documented.
- General processing design specifications should comply with the user department standards and procedures.
- The system should be easily audited and should provide processing integrity.
- Computer hardware, software, and time and personnel scheduling requirements should be defined and documented.
- If the purchase of new hardware and/or system software is required, the following items should be reviewed:
  —Lead times for delivery
  —Cost/benefit
  —Required enhancements
  —DP management approval of new acquisition
  —Scheduling requirements
- Estimated user and DP costs and benefits should be documented. Reasonable cost estimates of the following factors should be included:
  —System development
  —Testing
  —Programmer, analyst, and user training
  —Operations costs
  —Maintenance costs
  —Hardware and software enhancements
  —Cost of supplies
  —Development team manhours
- Procedures for security and integrity of sensitive data elements should be developed and documented.
- Interface requirements of this system with other systems should be defined and documented.
- The appropriate management should review and formally approve the general design. The development process should not continue to the next phase until this approval is obtained.

Control Objective. To effectively determine whether the software package(s) under consideration will suit the organization's needs.

TEST DESIGN FOR SYSTEMS UNDER DEVELOPMENT 63

Audit Objective. To determine whether the package evaluation process is thorough and complete and satisfies the feasibility study requirements and user specifications.

Audit Tests. It should be determined whether exact evaluation criteria were utilized:
- The package should be compatible with existing or proposed hardware, and its processing aspects should be practical.
- Feasibility study objectives should be satisfied.
- The user requirements should be an integral part of the package evaluation criteria.
- The benefits and objectives cited in the proposal should be satisfied.
- At least three vendors should be considered.
- Data storage types and access methods utilized by the package should be compatible with those used by the installation.
- The package should be capable of the type of processing required.
- The package should utilize state-of-the-art programming techniques and should be easily understood and modified.
- The programming language should be a type used by the programming department; if not, a plan for programming support should be developed and documented.
- Vendor support of the package should be an integral part of the contract for at least 30 days following implementation. Continual support of the package is strongly preferred.
- The package should have a reputation for reliable operation at similar DP installations.
- The total implementation cost should be approved by management.
- The package should satisfy all user requirements; if not, the required modifications should be isolated and documented. The cost for vendor and/or in-house modification should be determined.
- Modification cost should be formally reported to and approved by management.

Control Objective. To ensure that sufficient testing is performed to prove a package acceptable.

Audit Objective. To determine whether an adequate acceptance test was performed.

Audit Tests. The acceptance test plan and test results should be reviewed:
- Test requirements should be documented and should allow the auditor to determine if the package satisfies user requirements.
- The test requirements should cover all aspects of systems processing.
- Acceptance criteria should be documented and mutually agreed upon by the user and DP.
- The package's I/O requirements should satisfy user needs.
- The package should be compatible with current and/or proposed hardware and system software.

- The package should be capable of the type of processing required by the user.
- The package should easily interface with other systems or should be easily modifiable to permit interface.

Control Objective. To ensure that needed modifications to the package are properly defined.

Audit Objective. To determine whether modification specifications are adequately prepared.

Audit Tests. The modification specifications should be reviewed:
- A detailed list of the modifications should be documented.
- It should be determined that the modifications were prepared by the user and system analyst.
- The modifications and their associated costs should be formally approved by user and DP management.
- It should be ascertained whether the vendor or the in-house programming staff has been chosen to make the modifications.
- DP management should formally approve any in-house modifications or the cost for the vendor to make them.
- A plan for the completion of the modifications should be documented, including manpower requirements, estimated hours, and reasonable start and target dates.
- The user should review and formally approve all modifications, including those that will not be completed prior to installation.
- It should be determined whether the modifications will satisfy user requirements, system objectives, and system benefits; if not, the requirements or benefits that will not be satisfied should be determined.
- It should be determined whether the user agrees with the deficiencies cited and their effect(s) on system control and efficiency.

Control Objective. To ensure that a preliminary implementation plan exists and that it accurately reflects the remainder of the system development life cycle.

Audit Objective. To determine whether the remaining project elements are accurately planned.

Audit Tests. The adequacy of the preliminary implementation plan should be determined:
- All major events that will take place during subsequent phases should be isolated.
- Each task should be assigned estimated hours as well as start and end dates.
- Total manpower requirements should be established.
- A formal organization structure should be established, including an appointed project leader who has the authority to ensure that assigned

tasks are completed.
- A user liaison and other appropriate personnel should be assigned to the project team, with a commensurate reduction in their normal job duties.
- An implementation schedule should be documented detailing the start and target dates for each major task.

Control Objective. To provide senior management with a thorough and adequate recommendation, based on project results to date, that will allow them to evaluate the benefits of the proposed system.

Audit Objective. To ensure that the recommendation to management is complete and accurate in all respects.

Audit Test. The adequacy of the recommendation to management should be determined:
- The recommendation should explain how the objectives of the system and the benefits cited in the feasibility study are satisfied.
- The recommendation should contain the following items:
  —An overview of user requirements
  —An overview of the results of the acceptance test
  —A schedule of the needed modifications and their associated cost benefit
  —A preliminary implementation plan
  —Time, personnel, and costs associated with the implementation
- All elements of the cost summary should be stated in consistent terms.
- All time constraints and their resulting effect on the implementation schedule should be disclosed.
- Alternatives to purchasing the package should be disclosed.
- The recommendation should outline all short- and long-term benefits.
- Management should formally approve or disapprove the continuation of the project.

Control Objective. To ensure that the detailed design of the system to be developed in-house is complete in all material respects.

Audit Objective. To determine whether the detail design includes all material items regarding the system and operations of the organization.

Audit Test. The design documentation should be reviewed to ascertain that all necessary elements are included:
- The design of the system should be logical.
- All disk and tape files should be completely described and documented.
- File design should comply with in-house standards.
- Provisions should be made to allow independent audit access.
- Sufficient audit trails should exist.
- All required access controls should be included.
- All input data formats should be documented in detail.

- Input formats should comply with in-house standards.
- All source documents should be defined in detail.
- Validation provisions for the source documents should be documented.
- Operational controls for source documents and input should be documented (e.g., batching, balancing).
- Techniques for conversion of input data to machine-readable form should be documented.
- The completeness of the documentation for data origination and entry should be verified.
- The completeness of the procedural and operational controls over input data should be verified.
- Essential elements of the testing plan should be developed during the design.
- A conversion plan should be developed.
- Input, processing, output, and operational controls should be documented.
- System support procedures should be developed and documented.
- The detail design should comply with in-house guidelines and should be formally approved by the user, DP management, and senior management.

Control Objective. To ensure that the project team is adequately staffed.

Audit Objective. To determine whether project team members are sufficiently experienced and have adequate authority to complete necessary project tasks.

Audit Test. The adequacy of the organization and staffing of the project team should be determined:
- A project environment should be established in which all parties involved believe it is in their best interest to achieve the project goals.
- The project team should be staffed with qualified personnel from all affected departments.
- The responsibilities of each member should be defined.
- A project manager with adequate supervisory experience should be appointed.
- The project team should be organized by major operational functions.
- If the system serves two or more users, an official decision authority should be appointed.
- Milestones should be established to signal task completion and to permit periodic reviews.

Control Objective. To ensure that a detailed implementation plan is prepared and documented so that each member of the project team is guided in their activities.

Audit Objective. To determine whether all necessary tasks are included in the plan and whether respective time estimates are realistic.

Audit Test. The completeness of the plan and the accuracy of the estimates should be determined:
- All major activities in the preliminary implementation plan should be broken down into individual, manageable tasks.
- Each task should have a start date, a target date, and estimated hours.
- Target dates should be based on the estimated hours for each task.
- The plan should cover all project phases and the activities to be performed by the user, DP operations, and programming.
- These phases should include:
  —Functional specifications for in-house design or modification specifications for a purchased package
  —Programming, all phases of testing, and conversion
  —Training and documentation
  —The impact of hardware or operating system modifications
  —Terminal installation and forms design
- All personnel should receive specific assignments that are documented on the plan schedule.
- It should be determined whether personnel understand their assignments and are qualified to complete them.
- Required approval points should be noted in the plan.

Control Objective. To ensure that the systems analyst's instructions are adequately documented and cover all necessary elements of the system.

Audit Objective. To determine whether the program specifications are adequately documented and cover all necessary elements of the system.

Audit Test. It should be determined that program specifications are accurate and comply with in-house standards:
- Program specifications should exist for each program in a format consistent with in-house standards.
- The documentation of the specifications should be clear and concise to allow efficient coding of programs.
- All controls required by audit should be included in the specifications.
- The user should be formally notified that all specifications that have not been incorporated by this point must wait until after system implementation.

Control Objective. To ensure that programming is completed in an orderly fashion and that programmers are adequately supervised.

Audit Objective. To ascertain that the programmers' activities are well managed and supervised.

Audit Test. The programming phase should be monitored to ensure its proper management; it is important to remember that the auditor's function is only to monitor progress and point out weaknesses through the proper channels:

- The person(s) responsible for design and programming specifications should review the coding for compliance.
- Review checkpoints should be established.
- The programming job should be defined in the following detail:
  —Activities that will occur, together with their timing, duration, and objectives
  —The necessary resources, including when they will be needed and for what length of time
  —The end products
  —The functions of nonproject personnel
  —Change procedures
- A sufficient number of experienced programmers should be assigned to the project to ensure completion of programming within the desired time frame.
- Time estimates should be established for each programming task.
- Programming should be broken down into tasks that require no more than 80 hours to complete.
- A system of task reporting and control should be established, and status reports should be issued to supervisors on at least a weekly basis.
- A standardized approach for dealing with changes in original specifications should be developed; this must be in place to prevent over-budget situations and delays.

Control Objective. To ensure that all programs are sufficiently tested to prove compliance with specifications. This first phase of testing can be defined as unit testing, since it concentrates on individual program testing or modules.

Audit Objective. To determine whether individual programs have been adequately tested before the beginning of program string or jobstream testing.

Audit Test. Review program test results to ascertain the adequacy of testing:
- A program testing plan should be developed that includes the following minimum guidelines:
  —Test objectives
  —Scope of testing
  —Procedures for accumulating test results
  —A procedure for isolating and correcting errors
- It should be determined whether each program module has been tested and completely debugged.
- All programs successfully compiled and tested should be maintained in a secure central location.
- Controlled conditions and predetermined results should be developed.
- Test results that meet specifications should be reviewed and approved by the user and the analyst.

TEST DESIGN FOR SYSTEMS UNDER DEVELOPMENT

Control Objective. To ensure that all programs and system processing are sufficiently explained in the system, data center run, and user manuals.

Audit Objective. To determine whether system documentation adequately communicates the system function to analysts, programmers, and users.

Audit Test. The adequacy of systems documentation should be evaluated:
- A user manual should be prepared, containing:
  —Overall system flowchart
  —Transaction definitions, input formats, input procedures
  —Batching, settlement, and control functions
  —Output descriptions and each report's use
- A system manual should be prepared, containing:
  —Generalized system and program flowcharts
  —Computer setup instructions
  —Record layouts of all files
  —File retention, setup procedures
  —Index of reports, transaction code definitions
  —Internal and external controls

Control Objective. To ensure that all system functions have been adequately tested before conversion to a live environment.

Audit Objective. To determine whether all programs have been subjected to logical and organized test requirements.

Audit Test. The adequacy of the test plan should be determined:
- Testing objectives should be documented and formally approved by the user and DP.
- Program functions to be tested should be documented and agreed upon by the user and DP.
- Testing output should be predefined as clearly as is practical.
- Review of tests results should be assigned to specific personnel.
- A methodology for documentation and verification of test results should be established. This method should allow easy recognition of system problems detected during testing.
- A log of problems isolated during testing should be maintained.
- A formal problem reporting method should be developed to ensure that all necessary personnel are advised.
- Acceptance criteria for each test condition should be approved by the user and DP prior to the beginning of testing. Testing completion cannot be determined without this agreement.
- Test data should include invalid transactions that violate program edit and control procedures as well as valid transactions.
- Programs should be subjected to volume tests that approximate the volume expected in a live environment to establish processing efficiency.

- The final phases of testing should include all system aspects and manual operations.
- All appropriate departments should review and formally approve test results.

Control Objective. To ensure that the new system is implemented in a controlled manner (with provision for fallback to the old system should the conversion fail) and that all necessary personnel can operate the system.

Audit Objective. To determine whether the conversion will be adequately controlled to prevent the loss of data.

Audit Test. It should be ascertained that the conversion will be controlled and that all personnel can operate the new system:
- A conversion plan should be documented and approved by the user and DP management.
- Time and manpower requirements should be established.
- All affected personnel should be trained in systems operation and manual interface requirements.
- Management approval to convert the system should be obtained in writing.
- This documentation should be complete, including:
  —Systems manual
  —Operator's manual
  —Terminal operator's manual
  —Compiled listings
- Customers should be tactfully advised of any conversion that could affect them.
- The master and transaction files of the old system should be retained for backup.
- An alternate list of procedures to be followed if the conversion fails should be developed and documented.
- The last day's data from the old system should be reconciled to general ledger prior to conversion to the new system.
- Individual nonmonetary account data should be verified to the necessary extent.

Control Objective. To ensure that the system is turned over to a competent programmer(s) for maintenance and modification and that it will receive the necessary attention to operate efficiently.

Audit Objective. To determine whether adequate plans have been made for new-system maintenance and modification.

Audit Test. The plans for maintenance/modification should be reviewed:
- A programmer and/or analyst who worked on the development project should be assigned to maintain the system.

TEST DESIGN FOR SYSTEMS UNDER DEVELOPMENT

- After conversion, outstanding program changes should be reviewed to ascertain that an adequate implementation plan exists and that adequate priority has been assigned.
- The system should be running smoothly without an abnormal amount of operator and/or programmer intervention.
- The extent of user satisfaction with the system should be determined; any serious problems should be followed up with DP and management.

SYSTEM CONTROL ANALYSIS

The audit objective is to determine that there are adequate program and external controls to control input, processing, and output. The checklist establishes a base for determining minimum controls. Controls necessary for special system activities depend on the type of data and the processing method. It is the auditor's responsibility to single out specialized processing situations and determine that necessary controls exist.

This review closely parallels the application audit, with one important distinction: a development system does not provide physical evidence of daily processing activities; thus, the auditor is left with only an idea of what should take place.

This analysis should start in the early phases of the system development life cycle and should end just prior to the preparation of modification specifications for purchased software. In-house designed systems require analysis during the design phase and completion prior to the preparation of functional specifications. This timing allows audit recommendations to be incorporated into the system design rather than be patched in after implementation.

Test Design Checklist

A certain amount of information gathering must take place prior to the analysis of control objectives. The information-gathering steps are:
- The scope of the analysis should be reviewed with the financial auditors to obtain their input on controls for:
  —Transaction origination
  —Transaction entry
  —Program processing controls
  —Output controls
  —Information they need to complete their examinations
- The overall system function should be reviewed (i.e., a system flowchart and manual systems flowchart should be obtained or prepared; all manual interface points should be noted; and the programs, files, and reports should be labeled with the appropriate IDs).
- A list of transaction codes and an explanation of their functions should be obtained or prepared.
- Index reports generated by the system should be obtained or prepared; the appropriate explanations of each report's function should be in-

cluded. Those reports used for control, exception item processing, and management information should also be identified.

This accumulated data will form the basis for analyzing system processing.

Control Objective. To ensure that transactions are originated in a consistent manner, minimizing errors and controlling those that do occur.

Audit Objective. To determine whether the controls are sufficient to minimize and control errors.

Audit Tests. Transaction initiation controls should be reviewed:
- Manual or automated control points should exist to verify data accuracy.
- These control points should be defined and documented.
- Written user procedures should exist for:
  —Document preparation and regulation of flow
  —Adherence to cutoff times
  —Control over use of special codes
  —Description of input keying requirements
  —Input review
  —Authorization of input transactions
- The source document should contain a preprinted sequence number, transaction identifier, and all relevant data required for the system to accurately process the transaction.
- The forms should be designed to facilitate efficient completion.
- The source data generation function should be segregated from other conflicting functions.
- The preparer's signature should be required on all source documents.
- All input should be reviewed for accuracy by someone other than the preparer.
- Transaction authorization and approval procedures should be documented.
- Conflicting transaction types that can be prepared or input by the same person should be identified, and special procedures should be developed for their processing and approval.
- Each transaction entered into the system should be consecutively numbered for identification.
- A control desk function should exist to monitor the timely receipt of data.
- Critical transactions should be reviewed for accuracy prior to input.
- Large transaction volumes should be entered in batches and identified by a sequential number.
- The number of items in a batch should be limited to a practical quantity to simplify input reconciliation and research.
- Procedures to control lost data should be established.
- Control totals should be generated to prove the integrity of input.
- Transactions or batches moved between departments should be logged

TEST DESIGN FOR SYSTEMS UNDER DEVELOPMENT

by the sending and receiving department and controlled by transmittal documents.
- Input documents should be retained and stored in a controlled manner to permit reproduction in the event of a system failure.
- Retention dates should be placed on retained source documents.
- Source documents should be securely stored in a manner that facilitates easy retrieval.
- Procedures for handling errors should be documented, and the types of error conditions and correction procedures should be defined for each type of error.
- An error log should be maintained to permit follow-up and correction on unresolved problems.
- All source document error conditions should be reported.
- A means of cross-reference between the transaction on computer files and the source document should be provided.
- Computer reports that list input transactions for verification purposes should be generated.
- Corrected source documents should be subject to the same verification procedures as were the original source documents.
- Error correction and resubmission should be timely and should be monitored for timely resubmission.
- The nature of the errors should be monitored to determine whether they are caused by a condition that could be corrected.

Control Objective. To ensure that all batching input transactions are accounted for and properly handled to reduce errors, omissions, and lost data.

Audit Objective. To determine whether all transactions submitted are properly input and accounted for.

Audit Test. The controls over data entry should be evaluated:
- All data verification points should be documented.
- User documentation should explain the manual controls over data entry and prove that an adequate trail exists.
- Compliance with these procedures should be monitored and enforced.
- The data conversion operation location should minimize transmittal errors.
- Input operators should not be responsible for changing or interpreting data.

Control Objective. To ensure that transactions input by way of online terminals are subject to sufficient environmental control procedures.

Audit Objective. To determine the adequacy of internal and external controls over online terminals.

Audit Tests. The controls over terminal data entry should be evaluated; data entry, terminal security, and software and hardware controls should be considered:

- The terminals should be located in a restricted area within the view, and under the control, of management.
- Temperature and humidity should be maintained at manufacturer-suggested levels.
- The online system should be controlled by a message control software system that includes:
  - Password; terminal address; and transaction, file, and program control tables to control access
  - Lockout after a predetermined number of invalid sign-on attempts
  - Reverification of an authorized terminal operator
  - Operator IDs and passwords that are not displayed during the sign-on sequence and are changed periodically
  - Additional passwords for accessing or changing sensitive data
  - Assignment of responsibility for password maintenance to an officer in the department
  - Limited master or supervisor terminal status
  - Automatic terminal sign-off if no message has been sent or received during a certain time period
  - Polling of terminals to prevent unauthorized access
  - Reasons for invalid codes should not be explained explicitly in the terminal response. This will help prevent an unauthorized person from determining the input message format.
- Error edit override features should be limited or, preferably, not allowed; operator overrides should be reported for independent review.
- Terminals should not be operable during nonbusiness hours and should be protected with a keylock when not in use.
- Computer reports showing terminal activity should be reviewed by an independent group and should include:
  - Valid and invalid sign-on attempts
  - Operator name
  - Date, time, and terminal location
  - Programs, files, or transactions used
  - Computer action to invalid sign-on
- Dollar control totals should be used to balance input transactions (e.g., batch and accumulated dollar totals).
- There should be system and external procedures to allow correction of out-of-balance conditions between dollar control totals and accumulated input transaction totals.
- The line number, time, date, and operator ID should be logged for each message sent by the mainframe.
- The destination terminal address, line number, time, and date should be logged for each message sent by the mainframe.
- The mainframe and/or terminal should validate message format, including terminal address, password, message type, transaction code, and approval codes.
- Messages failing these checks should be reported by the system, reviewed by an appropriate person, and corrected using standard procedures.

TEST DESIGN FOR SYSTEMS UNDER DEVELOPMENT

- All messages should be logged on a tape or disk file for system recovery in the event of a failure. Multiple copies of these messages should be considered for critical data.
- Necessary audit trails should be created and preserved by the online system.
- Data encryption should be considered for data that would create an immediate loss if intercepted by unauthorized means.
- The communications protocol should match installation hardware and software requirements.
- Communications lines should be shielded and secured where necessary.
- Restart/recovery procedures should be completely documented.
- The online files should be able to be recreated to their original condition, including the last transaction received before the failure.
- File recovery should be automatic, with minimal manual data input required.
- System recovery/restart should be possible without the presence of the vendor or analyst.
- Terminals, mainframes, and disk and tape drives should be subject to routine maintenance.
- Spare parts for critical equipment should be maintained on-site.
- Maintenance personnel should be available when required.
- Downtime logs should be maintained for all online hardware components.

Control Objective. To ensure that the user and other necessary personnel have adequate instructions to operate the system.

Audit Objective. To determine whether system documentation is adequate.

Audit Test. System documentation should be evaluated:
- A user's manual should explain terminal operation, including:
  —Physical operating features
  —Message input formats
  —Response definitions
  —Key descriptions
  —Code definitions
  —Error response definitions and correction procedures
  —Restart/recovery procedures
- A system manual should explain system operation, including:
  —System/program flowcharts
  —Online system configuration
  —Computer setup instructions
  —File layouts
  —Tape library procedures

—Internal/external controls
—An index of reports
—Transaction code definitions
—Restart/recovery procedures
- The systems analyst should be knowledgeable in system operation and should be available when needed.
- All terminal operators should be adequately trained before using the terminal.

Control Objective. To ensure that all input transaction content is properly verified to reduce errors and omissions.

Audit Objective. To determine whether transaction validation techniques are adequate.

Audit Test. Program and external transaction validation controls should be evaluated:
- Critical data element input by means of key-to-disk, key-to-tape, or card equipment should be key verified.
- Preprogrammed keying formats and programmatic edit checks should be utilized where permitted by the sophistication of equipment.
- Check digit routines should be programmed, where sophistication permits, to validate account, vendor, or other critical data.
- The following validation techniques should be used where applicable:
  —Character checking (tests for sign, numeric data, alpha data, or blanks)
  —Field value checking (range, data consistency, validity, limit, reasonableness tests)
  —Date checking
- Processing schedules should be used to determine if all transactions have been received and entered in a timely manner.
- Source documents should be canceled to prevent resubmission.
- If batches are held by the program for control total checking, transaction totals should be manually or programmatically balanced.
- Terminal software should advise the operator when errors are detected.
- A preposting error listing should be generated to show errors detected in the transaction and to isolate all invalid data in the transaction.
- Corrected data that is resubmitted should be subject to the same edits as was original data.
- Manual or automated control totals should be generated for all rejected items.

Control Objective. To ensure that all data is accurately processed and the results of processing are accurately reflected.

Audit Objective. To determine whether adequate controls exist to prove processing integrity.

TEST DESIGN FOR SYSTEMS UNDER DEVELOPMENT

Audit Test. The integrity of computer processing should be evaluated, taking into consideration transaction identification, computation and logic, file maintenance, computer operations, processing error handling, reporting, correction, and resubmission:
- Each transaction should be uniquely identified by a code that directs the proper portion of the program to process it.
- Transaction codes should be documented in both system and user manuals that explain their function in detail.
- It should be determined whether all transactions function as documented.
- Internally generated transactions should be printed out for direct feedback to the user.
- Control totals should be generated for internally generated transactions.
- The control totals should be used to verify the change in the system balance caused by internally generated transactions.
- In certain situations, the system should control internally generated transactions with run-to-run dollar control totals.
- Control totals should be passed between jobs and steps when accurate file processing depends on previous processing.
- Overrides of programmatic controls should be listed on an exception report.
- To prevent access by an unauthorized program, system or application software should purge files as needed when processing is finished.
- Manual or programmatic balancing should be performed to verify the opening and closing balances.
- Computer operation instructions should be documented and should include:
  —System start-up
  —Terminal backup assignments
  —Error and system message explanations
  —System shutdown procedures
  —Job and system status reporting
- Run books should be available to the operator for each application and should include:
  —Console message instructions
  —Error message instructions
  —Program halt instructions
  —Rerun procedures
  —Checkpoint and restart instructions
  —Job setup instructions
  —Notes on forms
  —Carriage control instructions
- Error reports should be generated by the application and should include:
  —All data fields in error
  —Descriptions of error conditions
  —All information on the rejected transaction

- Out-of-balance conditions between batch header totals and transaction totals should be flagged.

Control Objective. To ensure that file access, file maintenance, and file handling procedures are adequate to prevent unauthorized access and to ensure that the files are protected in the event of disaster.

Audit Objective. To determine whether there are adequate procedures to control data storage and retrieval.

Audit Test. Data storage and retrieval controls should be evaluated:
- File library procedures should be documented for each application and should include:
  —Daily, weekly, and monthly job setups
  —File retention
  —File rotation and backup
- There should be separate production and test libraries.
- Access to certain files or data elements should be controlled.
- There should be software controls to prevent access by unauthorized programs or subroutines.
- File labels should be used to ensure proper file use and should contain:
  —File ID
  —Volume serial number
  —Creation and scratch date
  —Version number
  —Necessary security information
- Certain files should contain item counts and dollar control totals.
- The use of operator "ignore label" commands should be limited. When used, they should be logged and reported.
- File access and errors should be logged by the system, including program name accessing the file and the type of error detected.
- File journals separate from the master file should be considered to log transactions that update master files online.
- Reports should be generated showing accounts that have been inactive for six months; these accounts should be specifically identified.
- A report should be generated showing activity against these accounts.
- Files should be scanned periodically for erroneous data.
- All critical files should be routinely rotated to off-site storage.
- Recovery procedures should be documented.
- Files and programs should be identified as critical and noncritical to prioritize backup needs.
- File recovery and backup should be covered in a documented disaster plan.
- Logs should be maintained of all processing halts and operator interruptions. Operator ID, date, time, type of interruption, and disposition should be recorded.
- A log of all restarts by the operator should be maintained.

TEST DESIGN FOR SYSTEMS UNDER DEVELOPMENT

- Original and backup files should be copied when used to prevent damage to these files.
- All elements of the control language jobstream should be reported.

Control Objective. To ensure that all system activities and processing results are reported.

Audit Objective. To evaluate the adequacy of output reporting, including system activity and the controls over output balancing and reconciliation.

Audit Test. The controls over output processing should be evaluated:
- The results of the processing aspects of each program should be reflected on the reports.
- The reports should contain appropriate information to satisfy needs.
- Certain totals should be verified by an independent totaling routine at the end of program processing.
- The report should be generated in a timely fashion.
- A computer reconciliation should be performed for each run.
- The purpose and use of management information reports should be determined.
- Computer operators should not be required to verify or reconcile totals (except for processing completeness checks) before entering other files or continuing a long run.
- Data passed between systems by automated interface should be verified in some practical manner.
- All system interfaces should be completely documented.
- There should be an output control group in DP operations to segregate processing and distribution duties.
- The computer console log should be periodically reviewed for excessive operator interruptions.
- The logs should record each program execution.
- The I/O coordinator should monitor application startup to ensure that the jobs are processed on schedule.
- Report distribution should be documented in the systems manual, including the recipient, report identification, and number of copies.
- A control log should be maintained to prove report pick-up, including distribution time and recipient's signature.
- Reports should reflect all changes to the master file.
- The user should be aware of all changes to programs.
- All reports should contain run date, processing period covered, and generating program number.
- A listing should be generated reflecting all transactions processed, including internally generated transactions.
- Control totals reports should show dollar totals and item counts by transaction codes and gross master balances.
- Processing should be monitored for consistently recurring error conditions that may be correctable by a program or user procedure change.
- Errors should be corrected and resubmitted in a timely fashion.

- Errors should be identified according to type, cause, and source document.
- Error correction and resubmission procedures should be documented in the users manual.
- Error correction responsibility should be assigned to one person or group.
- Errors should be controlled to identify items requiring follow-up.
- Reentered data should be subject to the same input verification procedures as was the original input.
- Resubmission of corrected data should be monitored to ensure timely submission of data.
- The application system documentation should contain:
  —Generalized system flowchart
  —Program flowcharts
  —Run setup instructions
  —File record layouts
  —Tape library procedures
  —Internal edits
  —Index of reports
  —Transaction codes and their function
  —Internally generated transactions, their function, and the criteria governing their occurrence.

TEST PERFORMANCE EVALUATION

All phases of the system development life cycle are important, but the testing phase proves the success of the preceding phases and indicates whether the system is ready for installation. This phase produces the first tangible evidence of processing results. The auditor must pay close attention to development controls in the testing phase because corners cut to save time may result in a system that does not operate properly. The system controls purported to be in place during development are now specifically examined to prove their existence. It is vital for the auditor to determine that all necessary testing is completed.

Test Design Checklist

Control Objective. To ensure that the planned system is adequately tested before conversion to a live environment.

Audit Objective. To determine whether an adequate test plan has been developed and is adequately followed.

Audit Test. The test plan and the actual testing should be evaluated:
- The new system should be run daily as closely parallel to live conditions as possible.
- The user should receive all output and should verify its accuracy and compliance with specifications.

- User verification should be documented to prove that no report has been omitted and that all data is verified. If this documentation does not exist, the auditor should consider tracing a test sample of transactions through the system.
- The auditor should look for any extreme processing problems (hardware or software), document them, and ascertain whether they will adversely affect the converted system.
- The actual testing should reasonably comply with the test plan, and significant deviations should be justified.
- Test output should be checked against a schedule of what should be received to determine that all reports were covered.
- Test output should be compared with planned or parallel system results.
- All invalid test transactions should be rejected by system controls.
- All significant discrepancies uncovered during testing as well as the corrective action taken should be documented.
- A full retest of the system should be performed after the correction of any significant discrepancies.
- Test output that is not readily comparable to existing output must be verified by an alternative procedure. This method should evaluate all material elements of the new output.

CONVERSION PERFORMANCE EVALUATION

In addition to administrative controls, reviews of actual activities are vital in this last stage because of their critical nature. The old system, which created company records, is being replaced by a system that has been tested but is still unknown to a certain extent. Thus, it is crucial that data is appropriately secured from destruction or alteration and is completely converted. In addition, the new system must generate the proper control totals to balance system processing. Although accounting controls are important during the conversion phase, they may be overlooked by DP personnel.

Test Design Checklist

Control Objective. To ensure that the conversion will take place in an organized fashion, that the new system is operating properly and that all new files contain all relevant data, and that the old system files are adequately protected in the event of a new-system failure.

Audit Objective. To determine whether there is an adequate conversion plan and whether that plan has been followed in all respects.

Audit Tests. The conversion plan and the actual conversion should be evaluated.
- The testing results should be approved by user management, and the conversion plan should be formally approved by the user before the conversion takes place.

- All significant problems with the system that were uncovered during testing should be corrected prior to the initiation of the conversion.
- The current day's transactions should not be entered into the conversion programs. All appropriate files should be updated either before or after the files have been converted to the new system.
- If the current day's transactions are processed against the master files before the conversion, then the normal daily computer system/general ledger reconciliation should be completed and the master file balances proved before the conversion begins.
- The appropriate old-system files should be retained should the conversion fail.
- File control totals for the old and new systems should be generated for key monetary fields to prove that the files converted properly.
- Nonmonetary data should be verified through the use of item counts and item-for-item comparisons.
- The new-system files should be reconciled to the general ledger balances.
- Incomplete user personnel training should be completed within a reasonable amount of time after the conversion.
- All system and user documentation should be complete; if not, a formal plan and timetable for completion should be documented.
- Data center personnel should be familiar with all required procedures.
- All outstanding system problems should be subject to a plan for correction that complies with the normal system maintenance procedures.

CONCLUSION

The control objectives and associated audit objectives and tests presented in this chapter are, of course, not perfectly suited to all new systems; they must be tailored to the needs of each system. In addition, as with any audit review, auditor judgment is required. Using such tests, however, can help ensure an adequate system of internal controls.

6 Applications Projects Cost/Benefit Review

by Bryan Wilkinson

INTRODUCTION

In today's world, the cost of computer hardware and processing is going down. On the other hand, the cost of developing and installing new applications is going up. Prudent managers, therefore, are asking questions about the advisability of putting new applications on the computer or completely revising existing applications either to serve the users better or to take advantage of the latest developments in hardware. These questions can be answered by studies or proposals that outline the expected costs and the resulting benefits. Provided with accurate data, management can give the go-ahead to either lease or purchase the proposed application or to develop it in-house.

During the development or acquisition of the application, DP management is expected to have some sort of project control system operating to monitor progress and to ensure that the goals are met. Unfortunately, this is not always the case. An important audit objective is to determine how well this project control system is functioning.

After completion of the project, management should question how well project goals were met. Post-installation audits are designed to answer these questions. In particular, the objectives of a post-installation audit are to determine:
- The cost of designing or otherwise acquiring the application and installing it in the organization
- The cost of operating the application for a given period (e.g., an average month)
- Whether the planned benefits and objectives for the application have been met
- Whether the planned schedules have been met
- The causes of any variances
- What steps might be taken to ameliorate adverse variances and to minimize the chances of their occurrence on future projects
- Whether documentation of the cost/benefit analysis is adequate
- Whether controls designed into the system are functioning properly and whether some necessary controls have been overlooked

This chapter addresses all but the last objective on this list.

In some cases, a project involves both hardware acquisition and application development or acquisition. In such situations, it may be advisable to perform joint post-installation audits—one covering hardware and one software. The suggestions contained in this chapter have successfully been used to review several large projects with interdependent hardware and software implementation aspects.

INITIATING THE AUDIT

Not every applications implementation project should have a post-implementation audit. Auditing costs money, even if measured only in terms of the hours spent by an internal auditor. Therefore, the costs and/or benefits planned for the application project should be large enough to justify the costs of a post-implementation audit. Company or audit management may establish a minimum value below which projects are not considered for such audits. The effectiveness of this minimum depends largely on how well the project control system is functioning in the organization. If there is no project control system or if it is ineffective, the minimum may be set low. As the audit recommendations are put into effect and as projects become better controlled, the minimum may be raised.

The head of EDP auditing should receive copies of all approved project proposals so that he or she can assist in determining which projects should have a post-installation audit. If a dollar or work-hours budget is not routinely set for each approved project, communications lines should be established with DP management so at least ball-park estimates can be obtained. The absence of essential cost information should trigger an audit of the project approval. Limiting expenditures is difficult when there is an unlimited (i.e., no) budget.

Besides determining which projects to audit, the auditor must also decide when to conduct the post-installation review. Ideally, this review should be held after all costs have been incurred and the planned benefits achieved. It should not be so long after the project is completed, however, that documentation has been destroyed and undocumented occurrences forgotten.

Unfortunately, some applications projects have no true ending. There is a tendency to continually revise and improve. Whether this is considered to be part of development or part of maintenance is a debatable point. The auditor should urge management to specify a cutoff point on all projects—a point when the project is completed.

It is not unusual for a software implementation plan to show that several years will be needed to achieve all of the planned benefits, especially if the primary benefit is to reduce staff. The auditor should not wait several years to do a post-installation audit because the passage of time can complicate the reconstruction of developmental costs. Ideally, an audit should be performed no more than one year after a project's completion. The auditor should determine whether the benefits planned to have been achieved by the time of the audit are actually achieved. He or she should also estimate whether the existing controls and methods of operation promise successful achievement of all planned benefits. If the auditor does not wish to make this type of projection, the audit can be divided into two parts. The first part, an audit of the developmental costs, would occur shortly after project completion. The second part, covering benefits and reviewing any costs incurred after the first part of the audit, would be conducted when all benefits are supposed to have been achieved.

Planning Documentation Review

After a decision has been made to review the implementation of a major application, the auditor should obtain all relevant planning (feasibility) studies. A major concern is whether a decision to develop the application in-house or purchase an application package has been reached. If there is a formal project request procedure, the forms and supporting documents prepared for it should be obtained.

It is not unusual to replan applications projects. As the project progresses, additional information, which can result in altered directions and revised cost and benefits estimated, becomes available. All such information, whether formally approved by organization management or not, should be incorporated in this review.

Costs, benefits, and schedules contained in the plans represent commitments against which expenditures and achievements can be compared. The causes of significant variances from these commitments should be determined insofar as possible. Many such variances are the result of an inaccurate estimating procedure. This finding itself is important because management must rely on the accuracy of the estimates on which they base their decisions.

All planning documents should be reviewed for adequacy by an experienced EDP auditor, who will note the data to be included in the audit schedules. During the first review, it is convenient to highlight or underline with different colors directly on the documents any implementation costs, operation costs, quantified benefits, and nonquantified benefits. These highlighted or underlined documents become a part of the working papers and serve as backup for the audit schedules.

Audit Schedules

Four audit schedules are suggested:
- Implementation Costs Schedule
- Operation Costs Schedule
- Quantified Benefits Schedule
- Nonquantified Benefits Schedule

The Implementation Costs Schedule should contain the planned, nonrecurring costs associated with developing or acquiring and installing the application. These costs should be shown by type, described in detail later in this chapter. If these costs are to be incurred over a relatively long time, the planned expenditures should be shown by period (i.e., quarterly or yearly). The scheduled dates for such major milestones as completion of system design, systems test, and turnover to user should be recorded.

Slipped schedules can affect implementation costs. If there are revised plans and costs, the data from each should be placed on this schedule, preferably in adjacent columns. If, however, there are many revisions, the auditor may wish to show only two or three on the schedule. By recording the revisions to estimates of costs and schedules, the auditor obtains an overview of the changes that have occurred during the life of the project. Of course, any significant changes should be questioned, particularly if the documentation does not contain a satisfactory explanation.

The Operation Costs Schedule should contain the planned costs that will recur once the application is running. The auditor will probably want to record these costs on a monthly basis because that is the way actual costs tend to be captured. Again, revisions to planned operational costs should be recorded and significant variations questioned.

The Quantified Benefits Schedule should contain the planned benefits to which a numeric value has been or can be assigned. Items involving dollar savings should be grouped and totaled. These should be followed by other numeric values. As before, where revised plans exist, the changes should be recorded.

The Nonquantified Benefits Schedule should contain all benefits for which numeric values cannot be determined (e.g., items of improvement that are scattered throughout a proposal to make it more salable). Such items as "improved reports," "better information," and "increased accuracy" are typical, although the person writing the proposal is often unconcerned about their attainment. If nonquantified benefits change from one plan to the next, the changes probably do not represent true changes in goals; rather, they reflect changes in writing styles. Unless there is evidence that a nonquantified benefit has been eliminated in subsequent planning, all benefits, regardless of which version of a plan or proposal they appear in, should be candidates for evaluation.

These four schedules should be prepared in such a way that the actual costs and benefits achieved can be recorded on them. If the plan shows implementation costs and benefits by period, the actuals should be recorded for the same periods. If slippages occur, the actuals should cover more periods than the plan. The auditor should leave space on each schedule for costs and benefits not anticipated in the plan.

TYPES OF IMPLEMENTATION COSTS

Implementation costs cover one-time costs associated with acquiring or developing and installing an application. If a package is purchased, it may be capitalized and amortized. Since the Operation Costs Schedule calls for amortized costs, the auditor must decide whether to show such purchases on that schedule or on the Implementation Schedule. Caution must be exercised in

APPLICATION COST/BENEFIT REVIEW 87

any report that shows both implementation and operation costs in order to avoid duplication of capitalized costs.

The one-time costs associated with implementing an application can be grouped into the following areas:
- Nonrecurring vendor payments
- Systems analysis and programming
- Required hardware changes
- File conversions
- Forms and supplies
- User manuals
- Initial training
- One-time personnel costs

Not all will apply to every application project. The auditor may also encounter one-time costs not included here. All relevant costs should be included on the Implementation Costs Schedule.

Nonrecurring Vendor Payments

Costs of this type are incurred only when an application package is purchased or leased from a software vendor. These costs include such items as:
- Purchase cost of an application package or a one-time fee for an extended lease of a package (e.g., for 10 or more years)—Usually, such long-term leases can be extended at their conclusion for a nominal fee. The use of an extended lease instead of an outright sale is a contractual device to prevent the buyer from leasing or selling the package to others and to preserve the vendor's proprietary rights to the package. From an auditing standpoint, such a transaction can be considered a sale.
- One-time fees paid for enhancements and program maintenance—Such a fee may cover two or three years, with a monthly or annual maintenance fee imposed at the end of that period.
- Consulting fees paid to the software vendor or to others to help in tailoring the package to the organization's needs and/or to assist in its installation.
- Training costs paid to the vendor or others—These include tuition, other instructional fees, and the expenses of outside personnel.
- Manuals, forms, and other supplies purchased from the software vendor—These should include only the initial supply of such material—the quantity needed to start up the system. If several months' supply is purchased, the first month's supply would be listed. An average month's supply would be listed under Operational Costs.

Systems Analysis and Programming

If the application is developed in-house, this cost area should contain most of the costs. If the application is leased or purchased, this cost would vary, depending on the restraint imposed on the users and DP to minimize the

amount of in-house tailoring and enhancement. Costs to be considered are:
- Labor devoted to developing and implementing the application—It is advisable to record labor costs by type (e.g., systems analysis, programming, data entry, and users). User costs, in particular, should not be overlooked. Users may work on a design committee that helps establish systems specifications. They may review such design areas as input forms, output reports, and paperwork flow to ensure their acceptability. Users may also help design test data and review test results.
- Overhead (e.g., benefits usually assigned to the labor types listed).
- Computer time required to compile and test the programs.
- Computer time required to run the new application during the entire time of any parallel runs.

Required Hardware Changes

Some applications may require minor changes in hardware and/or communications networks. Extensive hardware changes should have their own post-installation audit. Minor changes might include such things as the addition of a few CRT terminals and data phones or modems. Costs would include:
- One-time payments to vendors for the purchase of hardware
- Delivery costs
- Hookup costs, including cables and cabling, communications line conditioning, and ports on the CPU required for the added equipment

File Conversions

As with programming, file conversion can be a minor or major cost. If the files to be converted are on magnetic media, conversion may consist of writing a program to convert the files from one medium and/or format to another in addition to the computer time required to accomplish the conversion. If the files exist only on paper, however, it may require a major effort to assemble all of the data and to enter it on the appropriate computer-readable media.

The steps to convert from manual to magnetic media follows (costs can be incurred at any stage):
1. Assembling the paper that is to be converted to a computer-readable medium (i.e., cards, diskettes, key-to-disk/key-to-tape, or direct entry)
2. Reviewing the assembled documents to ensure they are complete, accurate, and without redundancy
3. Keying and verifying the input
4. Scheduling computer time for the transaction processor (developed for the new application) to read and edit the keyed data and to prepare the necessary files and error listings
5. In some cases, preparing a one-time program to perform step 4 or modifying the transaction processor for the initial file preparation; also, in some cases, preparing a one-time program that will prepare the listing referred to in step 6

APPLICATION COST/BENEFIT REVIEW

6. Scheduling computer time needed to prepare a transaction list of all accepted input
7. Reviewing, correcting, and reentering all rejected input (i.e., items on the error lists)
8. Reviewing, at least on a spot-check basis, the transaction lists to ensure that the data is properly edited and that all required data elements are present and formatted properly

The steps to convert from computer-readable to computer-readable media include:
1. Scheduling computer time to print out the file to be converted.
2. Reviewing the file printout, at least on a spot-check basis, to ensure that the file is complete, accurate, and nonredundant and that all needed data elements are present.
3. Correcting, through the old system's (or systems') normal transaction processing, any errors, omissions, and redundancies on the old file.
4. If some needed data elements are missing, the same types of costs listed for a manual-to-magnetic media conversion will be incurred in the worst case. In the best case, the needed data elements may exist on several files. In that event, steps 1, 2, and 3 would apply to all files that will be used.
5. Developing and testing a program (labor and computer time) to read the file or files with the needed data elements and to prepare the needed file. It may also be necessary to develop a program for step 6.
6. Scheduling computer time to prepare a listing of the converted file.
7. Reviewing the file listing, at least on a spot-check basis, to ensure that all required data elements are present and have been properly converted and formatted.

Forms and Supplies

Although forms and supplies are usually thought of as an operational cost, the initiation of a new application may create a one-time forms and supplies cost and may also involve a one-time, larger-than-normal purchase. The following types of costs should be considered:
- The gross and new (gross minus salvage) costs of all scrapped forms, cards, and other supplies
- One-time (initial) purchases of disk packs, tapes, cassettes, and diskettes needed to get the application running
- Printing setup costs (e.g., plates and dies) for preprinted forms
- The initial purchase of application-specific forms and supplies (The auditor may wish to limit this to all costs over a nominal [e.g., six months] supply.)
- Racks and cabinets needed to store the forms and supplies (if not previously available)

User Manuals

User manuals describe how to prepare input, correct errors, and use the various reports. If the application is a purchased package, there may also be

manuals for data entry personnel and for computer operators. For in-house development, the data entry and operation instructions are generally considered to be part of the systems and programming costs. User manual costs would include:
- The purchase price of all vendor-supplied manuals.
- The labor involved in developing the necessary procedures and in writing the manuals.
- The reproduction costs of the manuals, including typing, drafting, and printing. If extra copies of user-supplied manuals are prepared, the cost of their reproduction should be included.

Initial Training

Users and DP personnel may receive training on the application prior to its installation and, perhaps, for a short time thereafter. Continuing training that results from employee turnover would be covered in the Operation Costs Schedule. Initial training costs include:
- Tuition fees and expenses paid to vendors for training
- Travel and other expenses paid to employees who attend training classes on the application
- The labor involved in designing the course and the cost of any training aids (if developed in-house)
- Labor costs plus overhead for all employees, both trainers and trainees

One-Time Personnel Costs

The few one-time personnel costs that can accrue when installing a new application should not be overlooked, including:
- Recruiting costs, including advertising and the travel of applicants
- Hiring costs, including agency fees and relocation expenses

EFFECT OF SCHEDULE SLIPPAGE ON COSTS

In DP planning, slipped schedules in application implementation are the rule rather than the exception. Such slippages can have unforeseen consequences.

If, for example, a new application is to result in a reduction in staff (a commonly cited benefit), every day the application is delayed is a day the organization has to pay the salaries that would be eliminated. These extra costs can never be recovered. Any other saving (e.g., supply costs) that must be deferred because of schedule slippages can be considered unrecoverable.

Slippage also directly affects systems and programming costs. For a constant project staff size, the cost will be twice as much if implementation takes 10 months than if it takes 5—a direct increase. Unfortunately, staff size may not remain constant. There is a tendency to pour more manpower into a project that is slipping. Some studies show, however, that adding manpower toward the end of a project tends to delay the schedule even more because of

APPLICATION COST/BENEFIT REVIEW

several factors:
- The new members must be brought up to speed by the existing team; this reduces the output of the current staff.
- The new members incorporate new ideas and directions into the project, thus nullifying some of the existing work. This work must then be redone.
- The number of communications lines in the team increases; this means that each team member must spend more time in communications and less time in performance. This slows development and increases costs.

A comparison of planned with actual systems analysis and programming costs gives some idea of the cost of slippage (or it may indicate the extent of planning inadequacies). The other costs of slippage mentioned may go unmeasured, however, and some may be immeasurable.

DETERMINING OPERATION COSTS

Some costs (e.g., annual lease payments to vendors and program maintenance costs) will not be included in the Implementation Costs Schedule. To get a true picture of the cost of a new application, the auditor must also review the operation costs. Operation costs are those that recur (e.g., monthly or annually).

When determining operation costs, the auditor should average costs over several months to eliminate the effects of unusually high- or low-cost months. A minimum of three months should be used. The first two months of operation should not be included, since these tend to be abnormal. People are learning to use the system, and bugs not detected during testing will surface. In addition, parts of the system may not be fully operational.

TYPES OF OPERATION COSTS

The recurring costs associated with operating an application can be grouped into the following areas:
- Vendor payments
- In-house maintenance
- Processing costs
- User personnel costs
- Miscellaneous cost changes

Where applicable, the auditor should determine the gross costs and the net change in costs for each item in the Operational Costs Schedule. Nevertheless, it is the net change that measures the impact of the new application. If the net change results in less cost, this saving should be included on the Quantified Benefits Schedule, whether or not it was anticipated.

Vendor Payments

So that the application developer can retain title, many packages have annual or monthly fees for use that may commence two or three years after the installation of the package. The auditor should obtain a copy of the contract and review it carefully to determine the required payments. The most common types of payments are:

- Fees for using the package—These are similar to lease or rental payments for equipment, and in some cases, vendor-supplied equipment may be included in the fee for the software.
- Fees for enhancements—As the package is expanded, the user may be guaranteed the use of enhancements by the payment of a monthly or annual fee.
- Fees for maintenance—No package is without bugs, which are generally detected by the users and communicated to the vendor. The vendor then corrects them and notifies all users of the changes needed. A monthly or annual fee is usually charged.
- Fees for special enhancements and consulting—A user may wish to have special enhancements developed, extensions that would not have a general market. Most vendors will perform this work for a consulting fee. The organization may wish to have other types of consulting work done or assistance in making the system more efficient. For such services, the vendor may charge a retainer or one-time fee. Such costs, after the system has become operational, should be considered a part of the costs of running the application.
- Fees for supplies and manuals—In some cases, the vendor holds a copyright on forms and manuals. Materials depleted by use will then have to be purchased from the vendor, or a fee may be incurred for reproduction.
- Fees for additional training—From time to time, the organization may have to send new employees to training sessions. Enhancements to the package may necessitate additional training. Vendors usually charge a tuition fee for this if held at a central facility. If held at the user's location, there will generally be a fee plus expenses.

In-House Maintenance

Maintenance costs will be incurred whether the application is developed in-house or purchased from a vendor. Vendors do supply fixes, which must be implemented by the organization's programming staff. In one company with a programming staff of eight, two programmers are assigned full time to implementing vendor fixes and enhancements on one package. The vendor sends a new set every two weeks. If the company itself had written interfacing programs and made revisions, the work would have increased even beyond the current high level because the programmers would have had to determine the effect of each vendor fix on their own programs.

Costs in this area include:
- Programmer time to investigate problems with programs developed in-house or fixes provided by vendors, to code the changes, to develop data to test the changes, and to document the results.
- Computer time for program recompilation and tests.

- User time to review test results.
- In worst cases, change procedures and manuals. All costs associated with these changes should be included.

Processing Costs

The net change in cost is of particular importance in this cost area because it gives management a picture of the cost effect compared with the benefit effect. This helps provide an answer to the question, Should the system have been installed? Gross cost, in contrast, provides an answer to the question, What is the cost of performing the functions covered by the application? The answer to this question has cost accounting uses.

Data Entry. This includes the labor to key and verify the application's input, regardless of who performs the function—user personnel at CRTs, a central data entry group, or an outside keypunch service. If data entry equipment (e.g., CRTs) is devoted to the application, rental or depreciation should also be included.

Computer Operations. This is the computer time and the associated personnel and overhead costs needed to process the application on a production basis. Many installations have a software package that captures such cost. If this is not available, the auditor may have to use estimates based on application processing time as a percentage of total production time.

Communications. This includes terminals, modems, and lines used for the application. As with computer operations, well-run installations capture such costs. If not, the auditor must develop these costs based on use percentage.

Support and Control Personnel. Support personnel are those people who decollate and burst reports and who may also pick up and deliver reports. In some organizations, these costs are considered an overhead to computer operations and are included in a computer use rate. When this is not the case, these costs can be estimated.

Control personnel are the people who receive and log input, review output for reasonableness, log output, and ensure that errors are reported and corrected. The cost of control personnel may be included in the computer operations rate or the data entry rate; it may be charged separately or may be ignored in any chargeback algorithm. The auditor should ensure that these costs, if relevant, are included.

Supplies. This includes bulk paper, preprinted output forms, input forms, cards (where used), and other consumed material not included under vendor payments.

User Personnel Costs

If data entry is done by user personnel, their labor is included under processing costs, which include the time and overhead (benefit) costs to:
- Prepare input forms
- Correct errors
- Review output

Miscellaneous Cost Changes

Gross and net costs should be considered in the post-installation audit. Three areas where changes in cost often occur are:
- Forms—The system may eliminate cards and reports, for example.
- Hardware—The application may replace one type of hardware with another, eliminate hardware, or add hardware.
- Salary levels—When data entry is moved to user areas, the persons who formerly performed a manual input function are retrained to use the CRTs. As a result of this change, salary levels may be upgraded.

DETERMINING QUANTIFIED BENEFITS

By determining the net change in operational costs, the auditor can detect some benefits that were achieved and perhaps some planned benefits that were not obtained. There is usually a timetable for benefit achievement because staff reductions, for example, cannot occur immediately after a system becomes operational. For this reason, the audit should be scheduled some time after a major portion of the benefit-oriented changes should have occurred.

When determining whether a monetary benefit has been achieved, and when the time from the plan to the audit is fairly long, the effects of inflation might be considered. For example, after a personnel reduction, there may be little difference between the total "after" and the total "before" salaries because of an intervening cost-of-living adjustment. This might seem to indicate that the planned benefit was not achieved. If, however, the number of reductions were multiplied by the average "after" salary, it might indicate that the benefit was more than attained. The auditor must determine how to present the fairest picture. The use of constant dollars is recommended.

TYPES OF QUANTIFIED BENEFITS

The proposal for a new application generally lists two types of quantified benefits: those to which a dollar value has been assigned and those without a dollar value. Although it is difficult to develop a comprehensive list of quantified benefits, some items can be used as a starting point.

Monetary Saving

Quantified benefits to which a dollar value can be assigned include:
- Reduction in wages, salaries, fringe benefits, and overhead resulting

APPLICATION COST/BENEFIT REVIEW

from personnel reductions—When evaluating whether this benefit is achieved, transfers to other departments should not be considered a cost reduction. Furthermore, any reductions should be offset by salary increases resulting from an upgrading in job level. Upgrading is a common practice when persons who were doing a manual, clerical job are retrained to use CRTs.
- Reduction in wages, salaries, and fringe benefits resulting from job-level downgrading—Such savings may be theoretical or deferred. The jobs may be downgraded, but, for various reasons, no wage cuts are made. The savings are realized only when an employee leaves and is replaced by someone new.
- Staff avoidance cost savings—This is another theoretical saving whose achievement is difficult to determine. Because factors other than a new or changed automated application can result in staff avoidance (e.g., decreases in sales or transfers of functions to other departments), the auditor may wish to give credit for staff avoidance only if a measure of productivity can be established. For example, if an employee who processed 100 transactions per day prior to the change now processes 150, a claim of staff avoidance would seem to be justified.
- Reduction in processing costs—This is another benefit that is hard to pin down. For example, reduction could have resulted from the mix of applications being run or from a reduction in the number of transactions processed.
- Reduction in the cost of supplies—This benefit is often claimed when data entry goes from a centralized group to CRTs located in user areas.

Nonmonetary Saving

Quantified benefits difficult to assign a dollar value include:
- Reduction in personnel—This, of course, is directly related to a saving in salaries, wages, and benefits. To give credit for personnel and salary savings would be to give double credit for a single achievement.
- Increased production per employee—This is directly related to staff avoidance savings and salary savings. Again, the auditor should be cautioned about giving double credit for a single achievement.
- Improved accuracy—Improvements in accuracy are often difficult to determine because of the lack of statistics on accuracy.

TYPES OF NONQUANTIFIED BENEFITS

The nonquantified benefits found in a proposal for a new application depend on the ingenuity of the person preparing the proposal and his or her judgment of what will sell. These benefits are usually not listed in a systematic way but are scattered throughout the text. The proposal writer may not even think of them as benefits but as "reasons for doing it." The auditor must carefully read the proposal and supporting documents to detect all of the nonquantified benefits, including:
- Better information, better reports

- More timely information
- Improved controls
- Greater flexibility in handling data
- Change from outdated to current technology

DETERMINING NONQUANTIFIED BENEFIT ATTAINMENT

The nature of nonquantified benefits makes it hard to determine objectively if they have been achieved. The auditor must use the techniques of interviewing, reviewing, and observing.

To aid in this process, a questionnaire should be developed based on the items in the Nonquantified Benefits Schedule. Users and DP personnel who might benefit from or be affected by the application should be interviewed to see whether, in their opinion, the benefit was attained. The two last questions on the list should be, Were there any other benefits resulting from the application that you have not mentioned? and Were there any unexpected problems?

If better data or better reports were to be a benefit, the auditor should review the before and after reports to judge whether there are improvements or not. Finally, the auditor should observe the processing of the application to determine, for example, how it has affected controls and the timeliness of reports.

Using these techniques, the auditor should be able to judge whether each nonquantified benefit was achieved, not achieved, or partially achieved. This judgment should be noted on the schedule and referenced, where possible, to interview results and reports of reviews and observations.

THE AUDIT REPORT

The audit report should indicate all significant variances from plans in installation costs, operation costs, quantified benefits achieved, and nonquantified benefits achieved. Where reasons for variances can be determined, they should be indicated. In some cases, steps can be taken to improve unfavorable variances, particularly with regard to reducing operating costs and obtaining more benefits. These steps should be recommended to management.

During the course of the study, the auditor may find major difficulties with the system. All such cases should be pointed out, together with any recommendations for improvement. Although this is not intended to be an audit of controls and procedures, some problems may come to light. These, of course, should be noted on the audit report, particularly variations that adversely affect controls, costs, or system performance.

A post-installation audit discloses how well the current project control system is operating. The audit discloses any important flaws in the system that have permitted unfavorable variances to occur and that could affect other projects. For these reasons, deficiencies discovered should be emphasized.

CONCLUSION

Post-installation audits may not be considered part of the responsibility of the EDP auditor. In fact, such audits may be no one's assigned responsibility. If there is no project follow-up, the auditor, as monitor of the use of company assets, should recommend to management (or to the audit committee) that such a program be undertaken. Examples of prior expenditures for new applications should bolster the argument.

When management approval has been obtained, a work program based on the material in this chapter should be developed. This work program should establish whether the information presented to management in the cost/benefit analysis was complete and whether the figures presented were realistic. It should also show clearly whether the benefits attained to date (and those projected) are enough to offset the cost of application development and ongoing operation. By following the work program, the auditor may uncover areas where large cost saving can be achieved through improved management monitoring and better project control procedures. In fact, the process of authorizing projects may be refined as a result of the work. Audits of this type place the EDP auditor in a position to achieve cost saving and increased cost benefits for the organization audited.

7 Auditing Application Programs

by Michael I. Sobol

INTRODUCTION

A publication of the American Institute of Certified Public Accountants, entitled *Computer Assisted Audit Techniques*, discusses the usefulness of the review of application program source code as an auditing technique. In addition to enhancing understanding of a program, algorithm, or group of statements that might be used in other programs, this type of review can determine that documented program controls exist in the source code, that the program reflects the specification from which it was coded, and that it complies with installation standards [1].

These are not the only uses of audit review of source code. By reviewing application programs, the auditor can also detect unauthorized or illegal changes made to the program logic; such changes can compromise existing controls or program results and/or contradict program specifications, objectives, and documentation. In addition, the efficiency or inefficiency of the design and coding techniques used can be determined. It is important to note, however, that none of these objectives can be realized unless management understands that the audit of application programs requires skilled personnel as well as commitment of time.

Programming Languages

To analyze a source program, the auditor must be totally familiar with the programming language used. The most widely used language in commercial DP environments, and thus the language the auditor is most likely to encounter, is COBOL.

COBOL, unlike many programming languages, is self-documenting to some degree. Comments explaining source code logic and procedures can be embedded in the code. This can be accomplished, in part, by using such meaningful data names as YTD-SALARY and MONTHS-TOTAL-SALES (instead of X or Y or Al or C5). In COBOL, data names can be as long as 30 characters. In addition, longer comments can be included within a COBOL program by placing an '*' in column 7; this makes a line available for free-form, uncompilable text.

The auditor must realize, however, that even with a programming language like COBOL, not all programmers write programs that are easy to follow. In some programs, in-line documentation and data names are of little help during source code analysis. Note that although an auditor may encounter other languages (e.g., RPG, PL/1, BASIC, Assembly language), COBOL is used for illustrative purposes throughout this chapter.

SELECTING A PROGRAM TO AUDIT

Before selecting one or more programs for analysis, the auditor should become familiar with the objectives of the application system by reviewing program and systems documentation and through discussions with systems personnel. Once a basic understanding of the system is achieved, several criteria can be used for selecting a specific source program to audit. These include:
- Purpose
- Exposure
- Frequency of use
- Life expectancy
- Availability of manpower
- Programming language used

The most important selection criterion relates to the purpose (i.e., functions) of the specific program. The auditor must determine how important a program is to the application system and whether it provides sensitive or critical data to management or passes such data to other programs. The degree of program exposure, which is usually apparent from prior audit results, and the overall risk associated with the application are important selection criteria. High-exposure programs should be chosen for source code analysis.

Other criteria that may influence program selection include frequency of use and life expectancy. Because of the complexity of source code analysis and the time required, it is important to focus on daily and weekly programs rather than on those that run quarterly or semiannually. Furthermore, if an application program is soon to be replaced, it makes little sense to devote audit time and effort to reviewing the source code.

Where to Begin. The auditor's first look at a program listing should determine when the program was written and by whom. Any descriptive comments should be noted. (In a COBOL program, this information can be found in the identification division.) The auditor should then determine what input and output files are read and written by the program and the specific characteristics of the files, records, and data elements of interest. (In a COBOL program, this information is located in the environment and data divisions.) With the program cross-reference listing, the auditor can then proceed to review the source code logic and controls.

AUDITING TO REVIEW CONTROLS AND PROGRAM LOGIC

The first step toward gaining a better understanding of a program, which is obviously a prerequisite to program control and logic review, is a thorough analysis of the existing program documentation. The auditor must be aware of the shortcomings found in most program and systems documentation. These shortcomings may have resulted from a failure to enforce documentation standards during program development and/or from inadequate documentation maintenance associated with program modification.

The best method of gaining a thorough understanding of a program is to review the program source code, section by section, line by line. Programs that conform to installation standards and that are adequately documented, with external documentation and with meaningful comments used liberally throughout the program, can be effectively reviewed in this manner. (See the Auditing for Adherence to Standards section of this chapter.)

Review of Internal Controls. An important objective of any audit is to test internal controls. Specific program controls can be tested by the auditor through observation, by submitting audit test data, and/or by reviewing program source statements.

The observation method has been used for years to review internal controls in manual and automated systems. The auditor should not be lulled into a false sense of security by this technique because it produces only a "snapshot" of information over a short period of time; it does not prove that controls are used continually, nor does it verify the internal logic and validity of the computer program.

The development and submission of test data is an important method of verifying program logic and internal controls. It has an advantage over other techniques in that it does not require that the auditor have a high degree of technical skill. Many test cases may be necessary, however, in order to verify all of the controls and validation routines within a program. This may prove more time consuming than a detailed review of the program source code itself.

Study of Program Specifications. The source statement analysis technique for reviewing program controls should begin with a thorough study of the program specifications. Such internal programmed controls as edit checks, hash control totals, and run-to-run totals should be defined in the program documentation. The programmers' instructions for writing the source code are taken from these specifications. The auditor must be aware that a programmer may accidentally or intentionally ignore or omit a control, and/or the specifications may not call for a specific control to be included in the program.

For example, a program specification may state, "Edit SEX-CODE for valid values of 1 or 2." The programmer, following these directions, may code the following data validation routine:

```
        IF SEX-CODE = 1 GO TO 090-PROCESS-MALE.
        080-PROCESS-FEMALE.
```

The editing in this routine is incomplete in that if SEX-CODE is a 1 (male), the processing continues for males; but if SEX-CODE is a 2 (female) *or any other character*, processing continues for females.

This illustrates both an incomplete data validation test and an incorrect default condition. The valid edit test would look like this:

```
        IF SEX-CODE = 1 GO TO 090-PROCESS-MALE.
        IF SEX-CODE = 2 GO TO 100-PROCESS-FEMALE    ELSE
           GO TO 900-EDIT-ERROR-ROUTINE.
        090-PROCESS-MALE.
```

A review of program source code would detect this control weakness, as would thorough testing using the test deck method.

Focus on Several Data Elements. The auditor may want to focus a source code review on one or more data elements (e.g., INTEREST-AMOUNT or OVERTIME-PAY). Such variables can be traced through the program with the aid of the compiler's cross-reference option (XREF or SXREF), printed along with the program source listing. The cross-reference shows all source program line numbers in which specific data elements are defined and referenced.

Flowcharting Transaction Paths. A traditional audit technique in a manual environment is to flowchart the path of a transaction through the manual system. For example, an auditor traces an order as it is received in the organization and follows the flow from workstation to workstation. The auditor inquires of those involved about each action taken at each step in the processing cycle. Such a walkthrough can yield an appreciation of the overall flow of transactions.

In a DP environment, it is not possible to follow a transaction through its processing cycle solely by following the paperwork flow. Many of the functions performed by clerks as well as the movement of hard-copy documents are replaced by computer processing routines. Therefore, to gain a complete understanding of the internal program flow and internal control, the auditor may choose to flowchart the program. This can be done manually or by using one of the commercially available software flowchart packages that automatically diagram program logic and data element use. Both methods allow the auditor to verify internal logic, observe the handling of arithmetic rounding routines, review built-in exception routines, and follow the flow of transactions through the program.

Automatic Trace of Program Steps. An automatic trace of individual program steps may also aid the auditor. The tracing technique helps by performing an electronic walkthrough of an application program. The objective

AUDITING APPLICATION PROGRAMS

of tracing is to verify compliance with policies and procedures by determining, through examination of the program steps executed, how transactions are processed.

Tracing shows what instructions have been executed in a computer program and in which sequence they have been executed. Since program instructions are analogous to processing steps, the processes that have been executed can be determined from the results of the program trace. Once an auditor knows which program instructions have been executed, an analysis can be performed to determine if the processing conforms to organization procedures and system design specifications.

Mapping. Another technique for tracing internal program logic is mapping. Program mapping can help assess the extent of completed system testing and can help identify specific program logic that has not been tested. Mapping is performed by a software measurement package that analyzes a computer program during execution to find out whether program statements have been executed. The software can also determine the amount of CPU time consumed by each program segment.

The original intent of the mapping concept was to help computer programmers ensure that programs were thoroughly tested. Auditors can use this measurement tool, however, to look for unexecuted code and anomalies in programs. This type of analysis can also provide the auditor with insight into the efficiency of program operation (see the Auditing for Efficiency section) and can reveal unauthorized program segments. Note that one or more of the methods discussed in this section can be used together to increase audit effectiveness and gain increased understanding of the detailed program logic and controls.

AUDITING FOR ADHERENCE TO STANDARDS

Programming Standards. Programming standards are designed to promote more efficient coding practices as well as more readable and maintainable program source code. An auditor reviewing source code for adherence to standards looks for specific coding conventions and restrictions that have been established and documented by the DP department. The auditor can test adherence to standards manually through line-by-line source code review or automatically by developing a filter program that checks each line of code for standards violations.

Some programming departments use a source code generator during program development; such a programming aid provides shorthand notation to increase programmer productivity. Many programming standards can be enforced through effective use of a source generation software product.

Examples of standard coding conventions that an auditor may be looking for follow. Although these standards are specific to COBOL, similar standards can be applied in other programming languages:

- Avoid large modules.

- Do not ACCEPT messages from or DISPLAY messages to the system console.
- Use comments throughout the program to explain processing routines.
- Use meaningful data names.
- Preface paragraph names with a sequence number, allowing room for subsequent insertion of new paragraphs (i.e., 010-OPEN-FILES, 590-CALC-INTEREST).
- Start picture clauses in column 40 and usage or value clauses in column 56.
- Try to make condition tests positive (i.e., avoid using NOT).
- Do not use the ALTER statement.
- Code one verb per line, and indent continuation lines to make the program more readable.
- Use all clauses in the identification division.
- Compile the final version of all programs with the OPT (optimize) option.
- Compile the final version of all programs with the CLIST or PMAP options for use if a program bug should occur.
- Compile the final version of all programs with the XREF or SXREF cross-reference option.
- Code subscripts as binary COMP fields.

Documentation Standards. The auditor should also be aware of program documentation standards. A review of a program for adherence to programming standards is not complete without a documentation review.

Program documentation for an application may be assembled in a program folder or compiled in notebooks. In either case, the documentation should be neat, up to date, complete, and accurate. Examples of documentation that may be retained for each program follow. Installations should select those components appropriate to their needs.

- Program narrative
- Source listing
- JCL listing
- Data entry instructions
- Operations instructions (including restart instructions)
- Change history
- Record and/or file layouts
- Sample input documents
- Sample output reports
- Test data
- Flowcharts
- Dictionary of data elements

In addition to installation needs for documentation, there are legal requirements that must also be satisfied. For example, Internal Revenue Service Procedure 64-12 explains recordkeeping requirements for taxpayers who maintain part or all of their accounting records in a computer system. The ruling in the Program Documentation section states:

AUDITING APPLICATION PROGRAMS

A description of the ADP portion of the accounting system should be available. The statements and illustrations as to the scope of operations should be sufficiently detailed to indicate (a) the application being performed, (b) the procedures employed in each application (which, for example, might be supported by flow charts, block diagrams or other satisfactory descriptions of input or output procedures), and (c) the controls used to insure accurate and reliable processing. Important changes, together with their effective dates, should be noted in order to preserve an accurate chronological record.

The auditor should check compliance with this and other applicable regulations.

AUDITING FOR EFFICIENCY

Another reason for auditing source code is to review a program for efficiency. Although computer processing speeds have increased dramatically in recent years, the system designer and programmer should still take advantage of hardware and software enhancements that improve efficiency.

Some language translators (compilers) are capable of automatic optimization of generated object code. Because optimization can significantly improve program efficiency, the optimization option, if available, should be an installation standard. If not available, purchase of code optimization software should be considered.

Optimization, however, does not replace efficient coding practices. Each programming language has rules and procedures that, if followed, yield optimal object programs. The auditor should become familiar with such rules. The following rules and procedures are drawn from COBOL:

- All numeric data items involved in arithmetic operations should be in packed format (COMP-3).
- Any field to be edited for printed output should be in packed format.
- One-byte alphanumeric data items should be used for all switches and flags.
- In testing many series of alternative conditions of data items, IF statements should be set up in the sequence of most likely occurrence. In most cases, 20 percent of the input occurs 80 percent of the time.
- Use of class test conditions should be avoided.
- Use of arithmetic expressions in IF statements should be avoided if the expression occurs more than once. Instead, the value of the arithmetic expression should be computed and referenced.
- Use of the ON SIZE ERROR option should be avoided in arithmetic statements by allowing enough integer places to contain the maximum field.
- Use of the ROUNDED option should be avoided in arithmetic statements. The manual half-adjust technique should be used instead.
- Because all calculations for subscripted variables are done in binary, all numeric items used as subscripts should be in binary format (COMP).
- The proper table-handling technique (i.e., subscripting or indexing) should be selected. In general, indexing is approximately 35 percent

faster than subscripting, since the addresses of the table are resolved during compilation.
- The SEARCH statement is more efficient for a small data table than is the SEARCH ALL. Conversely, the SEARCH ALL statement is better for a large data table.
- Communication between the program and the operator should be avoided (i.e., DISPLAY...UPON CONSOLE and ACCEPT...FROM CONSOLE should not be used).
- Use of negative compound IF statements should be avoided.

The preceding is a small sample of specific coding efficiencies that a programmer should know and implement in every program. The auditor, like the programmer, should be acquainted with these efficiency guidelines and look for them during source code analysis.

File design and access methods are also important efficiency concerns. The auditor should be aware that certain file access methods (e.g., virtual sequential access method [VSAM] and direct access) are more efficient than the indexed sequential access method (ISAM).

File blocking factors and record lengths can also play a significant role in program efficiency. Many DP installations use blocking factors that are tied to outdated direct-access storage devices. A major effort must sometimes be undertaken to correct those blocking factors to reflect newer, more efficient file-access techniques and direct-access storage devices. During source code review, the auditor should uncover such deficiencies and recommend improvements.

CONCLUSION

The review of application source code is an effective audit tool. Significant results and a greater understanding of application logic and controls can be achieved. Management must recognize, however, that to obtain valid audit findings and recommendations, a significant investment of time and skilled personnel is required.

Reference

1. The American Institute of Certified Public Accountants. *Computer Assisted Audit Techniques.* New York: 1979.

⑧ Auditing an MVS Operating System

by Robert J. Coyle

INTRODUCTION

An operating system is a program or set of programs that directs the computer system to perform language translations, manage resources, retrieve information, schedule and supervise work, and operate and control mechanized devices. It is used for creating and controlling the performance of applications it processes, and its major objective is to improve the performance of a DP system and increase the ease with which a computer system can be used.

The operating system is the major component of any computer system. It includes all system programs needed for a CPU to begin handling work. The operating system can be compared with the human brain, since it performs the thought processes needed to handle any given task. When an application program reads data from a file, for example, the operating system senses that a read is required and transfers control to the specific macroinstructions to process the read. The operating system then checks the program status for abends and error conditions. If there are errors, the operating system performs error exit routines (if they exist) and then returns to the next instruction in the application program.

In 1974, IBM released its most advanced operating system, the Operating System/Virtual Storage 2 with Multiple Virtual Storage (OS/VS2/MVS). This operating system evolved from the OS/MVT (Multiprogramming with a Variable number of Tasks) of the sixties and the OS/VS2/SVS (Single Virtual Storage) operating system of the early seventies.

The MVS operating system supports more users than does any previous IBM operating system. It does so through improved performance, security, and integrity as well as enhanced functions. The MVS operating system also has Dynamic Address Translation (DAT), a feature that employs a 24-bit address, allowing all users to program up to 16M bytes of addresses. This eliminates the storage fragmentation that previously resulted when real-storage locations were allocated to a program's storage locations.

MVS improves performance through the System Resources Manager (SRM), which controls access to system resources. Part of SRM is the Installation Performance Specification (IPS) member of SYS1.PARMLIB, which contains the computer installation's response and turnaround time requirements for specific groups of tasks. The SRM attempts to meet these requirements by balancing I/O-bound jobs and CPU-bound jobs to keep the operating system fully loaded.

MVS provides improved security and integrity through storage-protect keys, support for IBM's Resource Access Control Facility (RACF), and the Authorized Program Facility (APF).

MVS enhances the following functions:
- Job management through JES2, which replaced the Houston Automatic Spooling Program (HASPII), and JES3, which replaced the Asymmetric Multiprocessing System (ASP)
- Ability to select options and specify parameters during system generation (SYSGEN) and initial program load (IPL) to meet specific needs
- Addition of the Virtual Storage Access Method (VSAM), which provides a high-performance access method for direct-access storage

This chapter provides detailed information on those areas of MVS that should concern the EDP auditor and offers ways to review and audit these areas. The MVS qualities of improved performance, security, integrity, and enhanced functions are specifically examined.

IMPORTANT AREAS OF AN MVS OPERATING SYSTEM

The following sections discuss the more important aspects of an MVS operating system and detail the internal controls and procedures the systems programmer should install and use in each area.

Operating System Modifications

All modifications made to the MVS operating system, whether IBM supplied or written in-house, should be implemented only with the System Modification Program (SMP). SMP logs modifications into the control data set SMPLOG, providing an audit trail of all modifications. In addition, procedures should require that all modifications be recorded on a log sheet. This enables the systems programmer to easily identify the modification should the operating system experience problems after implementation.

The systems programmer should also be required to follow certain procedures. He or she should be required to complete a modification control sheet, which should detail the type of modification being made and the reason why. The technical services manager and the operations manager should sign off on this. This ensures that all modifications are authorized and communicates to the operations department the impact a modification may have on the operating system. The systems programmer should also assign a unique 7-character identifier, known as a SYSMOD-ID, to every modification for control and audit trail purposes.

AUDITING AN MVS OPERATING SYSTEM

All SMP output should be retained and filed to document the modification. Output from SMP generally includes the following functions: Receive, which checks the syntax and validity of the modification; Apply, which places the modification into the applicable system libraries; and Accept, which permanently places the modification into distribution libraries (DLIBs).

Critical Data Set or Program Access

All critical operating system data sets or libraries should be password protected to prevent unauthorized reading or writing. The following data sets should be read/write protected:
- PASSWORD—contains all system passwords needed to access protected non-VSAM data sets
- SYS1.UADS—contains information such as TSO user identifications, passwords, and level-of-access authority
- SYS1.RACF—contains user passwords and data-set-access authorization controlled under RACF
- VSCATLG (Master Catalog)—contains passwords needed to access VSAM data sets

In addition, write password protection should be assigned to SYS1.PARMLIB, SYS1.NUCLEUS, SYS1.TELCMLIB, SYS1.SVCLIB, SYS1.VTAMLIB, SYS1.PROCLIB, SYS1.LINKLIB, SYS1.MACLIB, and SYS1.LPALIB.

The following sensitive utility programs should be restricted from access by other than technical services or operations personnel:
- AMASPZAP or IMASPZAP (SUPERZAP)—These programs can alter data file contents.
- IEHDASDR—This is used to dump the entire contents or a portion of a direct-access volume. It can also change the volume serial number or initialize a direct-access volume.
- IEHINITT—This is used to place IBM volume-label sets onto magnetic tapes. It can overwrite previously labeled tapes regardless of expiration date and security protection.

System Generation Stage I Options

System generation, the process that creates the MVS control program, consists of two phases: Stage I and Stage II. The system control program is designed to fit the installation's DP requirements and machine configuration. Standard IBM operating system programs, options selected by the systems programmer, and in-house written routines comprise the system control program. Stage I of system generation can be viewed as the source level and Stage II as the object level or executable program following compilation and link editing. Stage I creates the input for Stage II, which, in turn, creates the system control program.

There are four important areas of a Stage I assembly where the systems programmer can select or bypass various control-type options: the control program section, scheduler specifications, TSO setup, and console setup. In the control program section, the APF libraries are defined. Scheduler specifications presents the option of a hard-copy log to record operator commands, system commands and responses, and operator messages. Which messages should be output to the hard-copy log is also optional. TSO setup contains such options as whether the full TSO command system will be included in the operating system, the number of log-on attempts permitted before cancellation, and the wait time between terminal responses during an attempted log-on. Console setup contains the CKPTREST (checkpoint/restart) option that defines which completion codes are not eligible for restart.

User Supervisor Calls (SVCs)

Depending on the computer installation's processing requirements, it may be necessary to include SVCs that are not part of IBM's packaged MVS operating system. These SVCs are referred to as user written and consist of routines developed in-house or software-vendor-supplied routines needed to support a particular software package. An example of an in-house routine is one written by a technical services department to provide added security features or special job accounting verification to MVS. Vendor-supplied routines can consist of SVCs to support CICS, RACF, data base management systems (e.g., IMS, TOTAL), and so on.

The system programmer defines the user SVCs during system generation in the SVCTABLE section of the Stage I assembly. User-written SVCs are numbered in descending order from 255, since IBM-supplied SVCs are numbered from 0 to approximately 130. In addition, the user-written SVC is assigned a type from 1 to 6. Types 1, 2, and 6 reside in the resident control program and types 3 and 4 in the link-pack area. Type 5 is used to reserve space for an SVC to be defined later. Optional characteristics for user SVCs are level-value locks, function codes to make the SVC restricted (APF authorized) or unrestricted, and the ability to make the SVC nonpreemptible for I/O interrupts.

Procedures should require that proper documentation on every user SVC be on file to adequately explain its reason and purpose, that the SVCs adhere to IBM's integrity philosophy and guidelines, and that SVCs performing restricted functions be defined to Stage I as APF authorized.

Critical Tuning Parameters (SYS1.PARMLIB Members)

To allow a computer installation to tailor the operating system to its specific needs, IBM provides various tuning parameters to MVS. These parameters are defined to the MVS operating system using various members of SYS1.PARMLIB, which minimizes the operator's need to enter parameters at IPL time. The critical SYS1.PARMLIB members are COMMND00, VATLST00 (Volume Attribute List), and IEAIPS00 (Installation Performance Specification).

AUDITING AN MVS OPERATING SYSTEM

By using the COMMND00 member, the systems programmer can have commands issued that never appear on the console and can specify which completion codes should not result in a program dump (preventing printed paper from being needlessly produced). A command available to COMMND00 is "Trace On," which provides the OS trace facility. Care should be taken in using this command, since it degrades system performance. It should only be used if the computer installation is experiencing numerous I/O errors.

The systems programmer uses the VATLST00 member to predefine disk volume attributes (e.g., permanently resident or reserved, public or private storage, suppression of mount messages). Procedures should require that only volumes that do not need to be mounted be specified and that attributes be efficiently specified. This will result in faster initialization and will reduce delay.

The IEAIPS00 member defines the computer installation's response and turnaround time requirements for specific groups of tasks. The SRM uses the attributes defined to this member to give priority handling to specified critical production applications. The system programmer should be careful to assign a priority to a production application consistent with the installation's ranking of it.

Resource Access Control Facility (RACF) Integrity

With its release of MVS, IBM made available a program product known as the Resource Access Control Facility (RACF). This product provides the computer installation with a data security mechanism to protect data files from unauthorized access. RACF protects both disk and tape files. Disk files are protected by data set name, while tape files are protected by volume serial number.

A weakness of RACF is that the Bypass Label Processing (BLP) parameter of the JCL can be used to negate security over tape data sets. This is possible because BLP skips over the internal headers on the tape and RACF requires the internal volume serial number.

The systems programmer can eliminate or control this weakness through the JES2 initiator parameters that reside on SYS1.JES.PARMLIB. These parameters provide the ability to restrict BLP use by jobs submitted through TSO, the system console, and batch (background) jobs. The following parameters are used for these three types: &RDROPSL for TSO jobs, &RDROPST for console-started jobs, and &RDROPSU for batch jobs. In addition, the systems programmer can write a routine that interrogates the DD-statement label parameter for BLP use and cancel the job for a job-accounting error.

Authorized Program Facility (APF)

Under MVS, IBM has provided the Authorized Program Facility (APF), which the computer installation can use to protect the system. System libraries authorized to contain APF programs are SYS1.LINKLIB, SYS1.SVCLIB, SYS1.LPALIB (only considered authorized during an IPL), and any libraries that the systems programmer defines to SYS1.PARMLIB's member IEAAPF00. A load module can be assigned APF authorization by using a PARM='AC=1' parameter of the EXEC statement when the linkage editor is invoked. The load module must be placed in an authorized library to be APF authorized. The APF facility then limits the ability to use a restricted function of MVS to authorized programs. APF-authorized load modules can only access other load modules that are resident in an authorized library. Attempts by authorized modules to access modules not in an authorized library result in a 306 abend. Attempts by unauthorized modules to access an authorized module result in an 047 abend.

Procedures should require the systems programmer to control access to APF-authorized libraries through a system password or RACF because any user can submit a job that executes an authorized program. In addition, procedures should require that:
- All APF modules have unique names.
- Volume serial numbers of authorized libraries defined to member IEAAPF00 are verified for correctness. This should prevent the system from accessing an unauthorized library having the same name.
- IEAAPF00 is kept current to accurately reflect only existing libraries and volume serial numbers.

System Management Facility (SMF) Options

The System Management Facility (SMF) provides an audit trail of any job processed by the operating system. Under MVS, the installation can select various options (parameters) to tailor SMF to its processing requirements. These options are defined to SYS1.PARMLIB's member SMFPRM00. The important SMFPRM00 parameters include:
- JWT—specifies the minutes a job is allowed to wait (e.g., awaiting a tape mount before processing can continue)
- MAN—specifies what types of records should be collected by SMF
- OPI—specifies whether the operator can alter SMFPRM00 parameters during IPL
- OPT—specifies the type of information to be recorded
- DSV—specifies whether data set and/or disk volume information should be recorded
- REC—specifies whether temporary data set type 17 records should be collected
- EXT—specifies whether SMF exits can be taken

The SMF exits that can be taken include IEFUJV (job validation), IEFUJI (job initiation), IEFUSI (step initiation), IEFUTL (time limit), IEFUSO (output limit), IEFU83 (bypass recording on SMF data set), IEUJP (job purge), IEFU29 (full SMF data set), and IEFACTRT (termination). The SMF exits reside as members of SYS1.LINKLIB or SYS1.LPALIB. These exits enable the systems programmer to branch out to specialized code if certain conditions are encountered.

AUDITING AN MVS OPERATING SYSTEM

To ensure that the SMF facility provides a complete audit trail, the systems programmer should specify that SMFPRM00's parameters have the following values: MAN=ALL (all SMF records are recorded), OPT=2 (system, job, and job-step information is captured), DSV=3 (both data set and direct-access information are recorded), and OPI=NO (operator cannot modify the parameters during IPL). The JWT parameter should be assigned a value that reflects a reasonable number of minutes a job is allowed to wait before being canceled by the system (completion code 522).

Program Property Table (PPT)

The Program Property Table (PPT) can be used to assign special processing properties to selected programs. This table is resident on SYS1.LPALIB as a CSECT (IEFSDPPT) of module IEFSD060. Programs can be given abilities whereby they:
- Cannot be cancelled
- Can obtain a unique protection key
- Cannot be swapped
- Can be made privileged (will not swap unless a long wait is encountered)
- Will not be timed
- Do not have to obtain exclusive control of data to maintain data set integrity
- Can bypass password protection

These seven properties appear in seven positions.

The ability to obtain a unique protection key is very important since MVS assigns these keys to maintain integrity. The keys range in value from 0 to 15. Key values of 0 to 7 are assigned to the system control program, JES2, data management, TCAM, VTAM, and IMS. All user programs have key values from 8 to 15. Programs with key values of 0 to 7 execute as authorized programs.

Procedures should require that only currently installed programs are placed in the PPT, with the reasons for special properties assigned to each documented.

AUDITING AN MVS OPERATING SYSTEM

The audit procedures listed in the following sections can be used in reviewing the internal controls and procedures for the MVS operating system.

Review of Operating System Modifications

To determine whether all modifications are being implemented through the SMP and can be traced to applicable control logs, authorization sheets, and SMP output listings, the following procedures should be performed:
1. The modification-authorization forms should be compared with the

modification log and the SMP output listings on file for inconsistencies.
2. Program HMASMP should be executed to list the control data sets (SYS1.SMPCDS and SYS1.SMPLOG). IBM's *OS/VS System Modification Program (SMP) System Programmer's Guide* should be consulted for the proper commands. Several modifications should be verified in the control modification log for agreement.
3. Program AMBLIST should be executed (see IBM's *OS/VS2 MVS Programming Library: Service Aids* manual) against SYS1.NUCLEUS member IEANUC01. The modification identification in the IMASPZAP data column should be traced to the control data set SYSMOD (CDS-SYSMOD) listing.
4. Several CSECTs from the IEANUC01 listing should be traced back to the CDS-SYSMOD listing through the modification identification under the user-data column (excluding those beginning with RS).

Review of Critical Data Set or Program Access

To determine whether all critical system data sets are properly protected from unauthorized access and all sensitive programs are restricted to use only by technical services or operations personnel, the following procedures should be performed:
1. Utility program IEHLIST, using the LISTVTOC parameters without the format option, should be executed against the system resident pack. The output listing should be reviewed for the presence of PWD (password) under the security column for the previously indicated critical system data sets.
2. An audit program listing the type 14 and 15 SMF records for any job using critical system data sets should be executed. The type 14 report should be reviewed to determine whether read/write-protected system data sets were used as input only by technical services or operations personnel. Type 15 records should be reviewed to determine whether only technical services or operations jobs wrote to the critical system data sets that should be read/write or write-only protected.
3. Critical system data sets that are read/write protected should be tested by using an IEBPTPCH utility routine to read one of the data sets.
4. The IDCAMS program (see IBM's *OS/VS2 Access Method Services* manual) should be executed to list VSCATLG (Master Catalog). The output report should be reviewed for password or RACF protection on the VSAM Catalog.
5. An audit program listing the type 4 SMF records should be run to discover any jobs that used any sensitive program restricted to technical services or operations use. The output listing should be reviewed to ensure that only these two groups used the programs.
6. An attempt to run AMASPZAP or IMASPZAP should be made to determine if access is restricted. The IBM service aids manual gives some examples of using this program with a harmless dump function.

AUDITING AN MVS OPERATING SYSTEM   115

Review of System Generation Stage I Options

To ascertain system generation Stage I options, the following procedures should be performed:
1. A copy of the latest full Stage I system generation should be obtained from the technical services manager.
2. The Stage I listing should be checked to determine whether APFLIB is included in the control program section. This indicates whether the APF facility is being used.
3. The scheduler specifications should be reviewed for the presence of Hardcopy=(log address, ALL, CMDS). This indicates that a hardcopy log is used and that all commands, responses, and messages are recorded.
4. The contents of the TSO setup area should be reviewed for the presence of CMDS=YES, LOGLINE=x, where x has a value of 5 or less, and LOGTIME=300. These parameters indicate that a full TSO command system should be available, automatically cancel a log-on attempt after x (five or less) tries (i.e., protect integrity), and give a terminal response every five minutes (300 seconds) during a log-on attempt.

Review of SVCs

To determine whether all user SVCs are properly documented and adhere to IBM's integrity philosophy and guidelines (as well as to ascertain APF protection of SVCs that perform restricted functions), the following procedures should be performed:
1. The SVCTABLE of the Stage I listing should be reviewed to determine the user SVCs defined to the operating system.
2. Every SVC should be traced to documentation supporting its reason and purpose. The technical services manager should give sufficient reason for all nonrestricted SVCs (FC00) and for any apparent excess of SVCs defined as free or reserved for future use.

Review of Critical Tuning Parameters

To determine the critical tuning parameters defined to the operating system, the following procedures should be performed:
1. Utility program IEBPTPCH should be executed against SYS1.PARMLIB to list the contents of members COMMND00, VATLST00, and IEAIPS00.
2. The output report for COMMND00 should be reviewed for the presence of COMP=. Determine that, at the minimum, codes 222, 322, 522, 622, and x37 are defined. This aids system performance, since abend dumps would not be taken by the operating system for these codes.
3. The VATLST00 listing should be used to test that all mounted packs have been defined and that the proper attributes were assigned to each pack (system versus storage pack).

4. The IEAIPS00 listing should be reviewed to determine which applications have been defined for priority handling and their assigned priority. These facts should be compared with the computer installation's current processing commitment for agreement. This will probably require consultation with the DP manager.

Review of RACF Integrity

To determine whether the computer installation is controlling BLP use, the following procedures should be performed:
1. A listing of SYS1.JES.PARMLIB's JES2 initiator parameters should be obtained from the technical services manager and reviewed for the presence of &RDROPSL, &RDROPST, and &RDROPSU parameters.
2. The fourteenth position after the equal sign should be examined for a value of 0 or 1. A zero indicates that BLP has been turned off.
3. If the value is 1, BLP is allowed. A program should be executed using a tape file as input with a label parameter of (2,BLP) to determine whether the systems programmer has written a special routine to handle BLP requests.

Review of APF

To determine whether APF-authorized libraries are password or RACF protected, that all APF modules have unique names, and that volume serial numbers and library names are accurate, the following procedures should be performed:
1. A listing of SYS1.PARMLIB members IEAAPF00 and LNKLST00 should be obtained by executing utility program IEBPTPCH. The listings are examined to determine the names of the APF libraries.
2. Utility program IEHLIST should be executed using the LISTVTOC parameter against the volume serial numbers of the APF libraries. The output listing should be reviewed to see whether PWD appears in the entries for the libraries.
3. Utility program IEHLIST should be executed against each APF library using LISTPDS to obtain the names of each library member. Members that have YES under the "Auth Req" column are APF-protected programs. It should be determined that all APF programs have unique names.
4. It should be determined that all libraries on the IEAAPF00 and LNKLST00 listings are being used by the system by verifying that IEHLIST output is obtained for each library. The accuracy of the volume serial numbers should be checked by using the VATLST00 listing.
5. Selected APF program executions should be attempted to determine whether they are access protected.
6. An audit program listing the type 4 SMF records containing 047 and

AUDITING AN MVS OPERATING SYSTEM

306 abend codes should be executed and the output reviewed for evidence of attempted compromise of integrity.

Review of SMF Options

To determine the SMF parameters defined to the MVS operating system, the following procedures should be performed:
1. Utility program IEBPTPCH should be executed against SYS1.PARMLIB's SMFPRM00 member.
2. The output report should be reviewed for the presence of the parameter values previously mentioned.
3. The value assigned to parameter JWT is then reviewed for reasonableness. An excessively small value will cause an unreasonable number of abends (522), while too large a value may result in degraded system performance.
4. If parameter OPI is set to YES (operator may override SMFPRM00's parameters during IPL), an audit program listing all type 0 SMF records should be executed. These records are IPL generated and contain a 1-byte field that can be broken into bits showing what SMF options were defined for the IPL (see IBM's *OS/VS2 MVS System Programming Library: System Management Facilities [SMF]* manual for further information).

Review of PPT

To determine whether only currently installed programs are in the PPT and if reasons for the special properties assigned to the programs are documented, the following procedures should be performed:
1. Program IMASPZAP should be executed with the DUMPT function to list CSECT IEFSDPPT of member IEFSD060 on SYS1.LPALIB. It may be necessary to ask the technical services manager to do this, since any SUPERZAP program (AMASPZAP or IMASPZAP) should be restricted.
2. The output report contains information for two programs on each line. This report contains four numbers to the left of FFFF. The first two numbers indicate the property value code, the third number the protection key the program will be assigned. The fourth number, a zero, is insignificant.
3. Once the property value code is determined, the auditor should convert the numbers to binary. A binary 1 in any column mentioned in the earlier discussion of PPT indicates that the property represented by that column is assigned to the program. For example, if the first position is a 1, the program cannot be cancelled. A 1 in the second position indicates that a unique protection key will be assigned to the program, and so on (see IBM's *OS/VS2 MVS System Programming Library: Job Management* manual for further information).
4. When all programs and their assigned properties have been determined,

it must be verified that the technical services department has documentation for each program.

CONCLUSION

Before beginning an MVS operating system audit, the auditor should review thoroughly the IBM manuals and learn how to use the IBM utility programs mentioned in this chapter. In addition, the auditor should write the computer audit program routines to access the indicated SMF data records.

This chapter identifies the more important areas of an MVS operating system and recommends the internal controls and procedures that should be established for these areas. Audit procedure steps are identified to determine the existence of these internal controls and procedures. The applicability of these audit procedures depends on the control philosophy of individual computer installations.

9 The Auditor's Use and Control of Utility Programs by Michael I. Sobol

INTRODUCTION

All DP installations have certain regularly used programs called utility or service programs. These programs have evolved from simple card manipulation utilities that perform such redundant functions as duplicating card decks and copying tapes to sophisticated programs capable of doing complex data and file manipulation, reporting, and modifying of existing programs and/or data files.

Utility programs are common to all DP installations and are intended to assist DP personnel in organizing, maintaining, and reporting on data files and programs. Utility programs are often employed by application programmers, operations personnel, and systems programmers for normal processing and maintenance. Among the capabilities of these programs are:

- Duplication—Data files can be copied or duplicated. This includes conversion from one medium to another (e.g., from disk to tape, card to tape, disk to printer, or disk to disk).
- Data modification—Records can be added to files, deleted from files, replaced by new records, or partially modified. These functions are of particular concern to auditors because they involve possible manipulation of production data.
- File deletion—Files can be physically erased from magnetic media, or space occupied by a file can be made available for other purposes. Utility programs can also remove evidence of a file's existence from system catalogs.
- Name changes—File names, library member names, or passwords that have been established to ensure data and file integrity can be changed through utility functions.
- Printouts—Data files and programs can be partially or totally printed or displayed on output devices. The output can be edited or modified.
- File creation—Data files can be built from cards, keyboard entries, or other input media. For example, test-data files can be created using the IBM utility program IEBDG, the output of which is a new file that can be used for testing production or test systems.

Operational problems are not unusual in the daily operation of a computer center. Utility programs are useful in solving these problems, which include unreadable data files, lost data files, unavailable hardware, and program bugs. When one of these situations occurs, the computer system may cease processing. The operator must then make several decisions regarding the reconstruction of the particular application. A well-organized installation has documented restart procedures for the operator to follow.

During these conditions, the sensitivity and validity of data is of utmost concern. If sensitive data is in main storage or on data sets that must be analyzed to locate the problem, unauthorized personnel (i.e., systems programmers or vendor personnel called to study the problem) may have access to it. To recover the data and/or application, the operator, vendor, or systems programmer may run utility programs to copy, modify, scratch, or print the data files in question. Such unauthorized access may not have been considered when security procedures were developed.

In addition, some vendors are now implementing remote diagnostic and recovery capabilities. Through online teleprocessing facilities, vendor personnel may be capable of utilizing programs from remote sites to manipulate data in attempts to solve local hardware and software problems. Local security and control procedures may not address the integrity of data files and program libraries under these conditions.

Utility programs thus are necessary for the ongoing maintenance of files and application programs; however, they pose a serious control problem. One way to control these programs is to eliminate them from an operating installation; but this, of course, is impractical. This chapter addresses the potential control problems of utility programs and discusses control and security measures for preventing their misuse.

REASONS FOR CONTROLLING UTILITY PROGRAMS

Utility programs pose five general control problems that require an auditor's attention:
- Unauthorized data manipulation—Utility programs can add, delete, or modify a record, data element, or even a character on a file without modifying and running the programs generally used to maintain that data set; thus, data can be altered independently of all normal safeguards. The program most feared among auditors, SPZAP (SUPERZAP), has these capabilities. (Control of SPZAP and other utilities is addressed later in this chapter.)
- Sabotage—Programs such as IEHPROGM can be used to destroy all existing copies of an important data file or a direct-access volume table of contents (VTOC). A disgruntled programmer can do considerable damage in seconds using such a utility program.
- Accidental destruction of data—Utilities are generally employed for one-time jobs. Because the normal checks and balances associated with systems development and testing do not exist in most utility runs, it is possible to accidentally destroy or damage one or more data files.

Unfortunately, the problem may not become apparent until days or weeks later.
- Overriding of passwords—Operating systems can restrict use of data sets to users who have the correct passwords; however, experienced programmers can override, modify, or obtain access to password-protected data files or to the passwords themselves through utilities. Thus, special controls must be maintained over password data sets and the utilities capable of overriding them.
- Bypassing system controls—Computer manufacturers provide a wide range of controls (e.g., passwords and file expiration dates) in operating systems to prevent the misuse of systems or data. Some utility programs, however, work outside the operating system in standalone mode and are able to bypass these controls. If an installation relies on IBM's System Management Facility (SMF) to record access to data sets, for example, the SMF records can be incomplete if a utility program is run in standalone mode or if SMF is deactivated.

Although this list is not exhaustive, it represents some problems that may be encountered. The advantages of using certain software packages must continually be evaluated in relation to the inherent risks. Since the advantages associated with utilities usually outweigh the dangers, the auditor must ensure that adequate control and security measures have been provided to reduce the risk of misusing them.

The potential risks created by utilities may be symptomatic of other problems:
- The misuse of utility programs may indicate a lack of adequate control procedures in other audit areas. A review of the reasons for the use of utility programs may reveal this lack.
- Excessive use of utility programs may indicate that application programmers, systems programmers, or operations personnel rely on utility programs as a crutch or as a permanent fix for recurring problems. This may not be an effective use of utility programs.

UTILITY PROGRAM AUDITS

The audit of utility programs helps the auditor understand their capabilities and how they can be used to conduct audits more efficiently and effectively in other areas of the DP organization.

One approach to conducting a utility program audit is to combine interviews of personnel with reviews of systems documentation. The interviews should be conducted with systems programmer personnel, operations personnel, and application programmers. Each group's use of the various utilities should be reviewed. More reliable sources of information are the audit trails produced by the system (e.g., the systems console log and the SMF data). Both sources record the use of utility programs.

The overall audit objective is to determine the following:
- Specific programs used—This question can be answered best through a

review of the system console log or the SMF data.
- Access—Because of their capabilities and potential for exposure, utility programs should be restricted to selected operations/systems personnel. The auditor should determine who has access.
- Circumstances of use—Although SMF and the systems log record all program execution, they do not report when an embedded utility program (subprogram) is used or when a standalone or independent utility program is executed without the operating system. (Entrance/exit routines can be built into some utilities for further control.) With these exceptions, the console log or SMF data can yield information informing when these utilities are used.
- Frequency of use—Certain utility programs have special features for emergency situations. Frequent use of these programs indicates that problems of a serious nature occur too often.
- Controls governing use—Not all utility programs require the same level of control. The auditor must exercise judgment in evaluating the adequacy of controls. It must be decided whether strict access controls are necessary or whether the systems log or the SMF data (after-the-fact logs) is sufficient to monitor utility program use.
- Effectiveness of controls—The auditor can test to determine whether existing controls are working effectively. Running a utility program to list passwords in the password data set, listing information in sensitive files, or modifying restricted data are examples. If these tests prove that controls are lacking, a tightening of systems security is warranted.

As operations procedures vary widely among installations, so do control practices, especially for utility programs. The utility program audit points to areas where increased control and security measures should be implemented.

How to Evaluate Controls over Utilities

Utility programs can be categorized into those that have little or no effect on secure information (low risk) and those that modify and/or report on sensitive and secure information (high risk). The following steps should be taken when developing controls:
- List and rank according to potential exposure all utility programs available at the installation. Utilities developed in-house or received from other installations can pose a greater hazard than do standard vendor utilities. High-risk programs should be removed from the standard utility library and placed in a restricted utility program library, subject to password control. Only authorized individuals should be able to enter the password.
- Establish password controls over data files. These files should be accessed only by authorized users who can transmit a correct password. This file control should apply to all DP operations to provide tight control over the misuse of utilities and protect sensitive data from exposure.
- Periodically review the systems log and the SMF data to see which

USE AND CONTROL OF UTILITY PROGRAMS

utility programs are being used, who is using them, and what files are being accessed. These reviews make computer personnel aware that management is serious in its efforts to control and monitor utility-program use.
* Monitor all program execution. Exit routines can be written into SMF modules, and high-risk programs, users, and data files can be identified and execution canceled in case of a violation.

UTILITY PROGRAMS FOR AUDITOR'S USE

Utility programs provide much of the data that auditors need. In addition, utilities can perform many tasks handled by audit software, with a few exceptions (e.g., statistical sampling and graphic output). Although good working knowledge of DP is necessary to use these programs, utilities can often operate and provide data more economically and with greater capability than can many computer-audit software systems.

Although the examples in this chapter are from the IBM OS product line, computer vendors have extensive utility program libraries. Non-IBM users should find direct parallels in the utility programs provided by their particular vendor.

Entry-List Utility

IEHLIST is used to list entries in a catalog, in the directory of one or more partitioned data sets (PDS), or in a VTOC. This utility provides three reports useful for a data-center audit.

Catalog Entries. IEHLIST lists all entries in a systems catalog. The entries indicate the vendor and production data sets cataloged on the system.

Directory Entries. IEHLIST prints the directory entries for a PDS. Each PDS member is listed, along with information useful for auditing purposes. If a PDS contains load modules produced by the OS linkage editor, for example, information such as the virtual-storage size of the load module, starting address of the PDS member, System Status Indicator (SSI), and Authorized Program Facility (APF) code are printed. The auditor can use this information to determine changes to production-load modules, version and modification number of system modules, and authorization levels of individual programs.

During an audit of program changes, if the size of a load module or the address of the load module in the PDS changes, this indicates that a recompilation and link-edit of a program took place and that the load module may have been modified during the interval being tested. Under these circumstances, the auditor should review the supporting program-change documentation to validate the change. This should include a review of maintenance requests from users; DP procedures to control the change; and testing, review, and authorization procedures.

VTOC. IEHLIST can also be used to list a disk's VTOC. The VTOC consists of as many as seven types of data-set control blocks (DSCBs) containing information about the data sets residing on the volume. The auditor also receives information about:
- Characteristics of the volume (e.g., the number of alternate tracks in use)
- Location of the VTOC
- Amount of free space on the volume
- Name and location of each data file
- Creation date of each data set
- Expiration date of each data set
- File organization
- Evidence of password-protection use for files on the volume

This VTOC information provides an overall view of the efficiency and effectiveness of the direct-access storage device's use as well as an indication of access controls in effect.

Modification Utility

IEHPROGM is used to modify system control data sets and to maintain files at an organizational level. IEHPROGM can be used to scratch a data set or member, rename a data set or member, and maintain data set passwords. In addition, it can be used to scratch the following from a direct-access volume: the VTOC, a specific data set, a member of a partitioned data set, and password-protected data sets. It can also scratch work data sets left by the operating system. The utility can override the expiration-date control established to prevent unauthorized writing to a data set.

Because IEHPROGM's powerful commands can severely damage a volume, it should be used only by authorized personnel. Moreover, strict control and monitoring must be maintained over its use.

Build Data Generator

IEBDG is used to create a pattern of test data to be used by programmers as a debugging aid or by auditors in testing new or modified programs or systems. The utility program can generate test-data records in any format, and existing data sets can be used as input by selecting portions of records for inclusion in records in the output-generated test file.

In addition to user-supplied input records, the utility can provide up to seven data formats: alphanumeric, alphabetic, zoned decimal, packed decimal, binary numbers, collating sequence numbers, and random numbers. The programmer or auditor can choose one of these formats for the content of each field defined. A pattern can be chosen that varies the content from record to record. By using existing records in combination with the supplied formats, the auditor can generate an entirely new data set, suitable for testing changes made to existing systems or for thoroughly testing the various logic paths and edit routines of a new system.

USE AND CONTROL OF UTILITY PROGRAMS

Copy Utility

IEBCOPY is used to copy one or more partitioned data sets or to merge partitioned data sets. A partitioned data set copied to a sequential file (e.g., a tape) is said to be unloaded. The magnetic-tape data set created by this unload operation can be copied to other direct-access devices. Recreating a partitioned data set from one or more unloaded data sets is termed a load operation. Unloading and loading partitioned data sets are a means of creating backup copies of critical library files. The utility program allows specific members of a partitioned data set or an unloaded PDS to be selected or excluded from a copy, unload, or load operation.

This program is useful for making copies of production library files under audit control. Once these libraries have been copied, special runs to test individual programs can be made, using the controlled programs from the auditor's library.

Print/Punch Utility

IEBPTPCH is used to print or punch all or selected portions of a sequential or partitioned data set. Auditors can use it to list the contents of files or PDS members containing test data, JCL, or parameters used by the operating system. IEBPTPCH cannot be used to print the contents of PDS members containing load modules. (AMBLIST, discussed later in this chapter, can be used to print load modules.)

Generate Utility

IEBGENER is used to create a backup copy of a data set or a partitioned data set member and to print the contents of a partitioned data set member. The auditor thus can use this utility to produce backup copies of data sets and the contents of partitioned data set members (e.g., JCL from a procedure library, source statements from a source library, or systems parameters from a systems parameter library).

Initialization Utility

IEHINITT is used to place IBM standard volume labels on magnetic tapes. Because IEHINITT can overwrite previously labeled tapes, regardless of expiration date and password security, this program creates unusually high-risk exposure.

To control this utility and prevent unauthorized destruction of standard labeled tape files, it is suggested that IEHINITT be removed from the system library (SYS1.LINKLIB) and placed in an authorized password-protected library.

All-Purpose Utilities

The programs DEBE/DITTO are not formally supported IBM utility programs. They have been developed over the years and passed among installations through SHARE and GUIDE library services. Both perform similar functions and are often invoked from the operator console. They are popular because of their ease of execution and the flexibility and power of the services provided.

One danger in these programs is their ability to modify individual records, data elements, or bytes on direct-access storage devices. A computer operator could, through the operator console, invoke DITTO and change specific fields on master files or modify production programs (load modules).

These programs, like SPZAP, are invaluable tools for operations personnel and therefore cannot be removed from the system; but controls, such as those discussed earlier, must be in place to monitor use and protect sensitive data and program files.

Assembly Module Utility

The IBM service aid program AMBLIST is designed for use by systems programmers in performing diagnostic functions (e.g., verifying an object module, mapping control sections in a load module, and tracing modifications to the executable code in a control section).

Although not intended for general use, this program provides some vital information for auditing. For example, by listing a load module's identification record (IDR), the auditor can determine the date the load module was link edited. This information is useful in detecting unauthorized changes to programs. In addition, the IDR gives the date of load module modifications made by SPZAP. This information is useful in determining whether the program was patched or modified with the SPZAP service program.

Service Program

The SPZAP (SUPERZAP) service program is designed to enable personnel to:

- Inspect and modify instructions and data in any load module that is a member of a partitioned data set
- Inspect and modify data in a specific record in a direct-access data set
- Dump an entire data set, member of a PDS, or any portion of a data set residing on a direct-access device
- Update the SSI in the directory of any load module

From an auditor's viewpoint, the SPZAP program is the most dangerous utility because it has the power to patch load modules and circumvent built-in change controls. It is frequently used to make emergency fixes to programs so that execution can continue as quickly as possible following a program failure. In addition, SPZAP is used regularly by IBM to apply program fixes to system modules.

SPZAP leaves an audit-trail date in any load module it updates. This can be reviewed by executing AMBLIST as previously described. In addition, SPZAP updates a load-module SSI, which can be used to keep track of any modifications that are performed on a load module.

USE AND CONTROL OF UTILITY PROGRAMS

Because SPZAP can modify data on a direct-access storage device, misuse can result in serious damage to user and system load modules or data sets. Two facilities for controlling SPZAP in order to guard against such damage are:

- SMF—This provides system interface with user exit routines in order to monitor the jobstream. This facility, when incorporated into the system, affords an internal means of determining whether a particular user is authorized to execute the program specified on the EXEC JCL statement.
- Password-protected library—Storing SPZAP in such a library requires anyone attempting to execute it to include in the JCL statements a JOBLIB DD statement defining the library. In addition, the correct password is required at execution time to gain access to the program.

CONCLUSION

Utility and service programs provide fast, easy access to system and production data sets and programs. Audit personnel can use them to monitor data center operations and to assist in testing control procedures.

In addition to these benefits, however, several utility and service programs have capabilities that, if used maliciously, can cause serious problems. The auditor must not only take advantage of utility program capabilities but must ensure that the proper control and security measures are in place to prevent their misuse.

10 Auditing JCL Standards

by Steven F. Blanding

INTRODUCTION

Command languages or job control languages are used to define the tasks performed by a computer. The term "command language" is generally associated with interactive or time-sharing systems, while "job control language" is used primarily with batch processing systems. In most cases, these languages interact with the computer's operating system to request resources in performing tasks (or jobs). The operating system acts as a monitor to control resources, thus increasing computer efficiency.

Early computer systems could execute only one job at a time and did not use an operating system. The operator was in total control of the execution of the job and thus the operation of the entire system. As computers became more complex, simple operating systems and job control languages were developed to assist operators in performing their duties.

With the development of multiprogramming operating systems, several independent tasks could be executed simultaneously. Because of these capabilities, the operator or programmer had to request resources in a more detailed and rigorous fashion. Job control languages became more complex as the definition of jobs to the operating system became more precise.

Currently, operators or programmers use highly complex and powerful job control languages to:
- Identify themselves to the system for accounting and security purposes and to request the data files needed to process their respective jobs
- Inform the computer about the resources required (e.g., amounts of primary and secondary storage, compilers to be used, and expected amount of central processing time for each program)
- Specify the I/O devices required by their respective jobs (e.g., magnetic tapes, disks, and line printers) and to define the manner in which the data is formatted on these peripheral devices
- Specify what action the computer should take in exceptional cases (e.g., ABENDS, errors in programs, missing or incorrect input data, and I/O device failures)

Although the operating system is responsible for managing all resources of the computer system, the requirements for those resources can be modified by the job control languages, of which there are two types. Statement-oriented languages comprise a large number of statements, each containing a small number of parameters; parameter-oriented languages are composed of a small number of statements in which a large number of parameters are grouped.

The power and versatility of the statements are evidenced through the use of JCL parameters. Extensive use of positioned and keyword parameters adds to the complexity of the language. Positional parameters must appear in a specified order on the JCL statement. Keyword parameters consist of a keyword followed by one or more values and must follow any positional parameters coded in the statement.

By assigning values to positional and keyword parameters in a job, a programmer or operator can, for example, determine a job's scheduling priority over other jobs in the system. The programmer can also specify additional core storage for the execution of a program within a job or set a limit on the amount of core. In essence, the capability to request computer resources and services through JCL is limited only by the capability of the computer itself.

Audit Approach

Most computer installations use standards to some degree to control the use of JCL. These standards are determined by the values assigned to positional and keyword parameters. Standards are also established by the relationship between values of different parameters.

JCL standards must be audited because they are used to:
- Prevent unauthorized use of the computer
- Support naming conventions that are part of the overall computer installation documentation standards
- Support computer charge-out systems and computer resource and efficiency planning

Because auditing JCL standards requires an in-depth understanding of the JCL used in the data center, the auditor should review vendor manuals and consult with systems programming personnel. Once he or she understands the capabilities of the JCL, the auditor should determine whether the installation has established standards for its use. Written standards should be incorporated with the data center standards manual.

The auditor should review and evaluate the standards to determine whether they adequately support the control of computer resources and the efficiency of the operating system. Depending on the capabilities of the JCL in use, this support would include:
- Specifying realistic space allocations
- Making the jobs independent of devices, where possible
- Ensuring conflicts do not occur between data sets (data set naming conventions and generation data sets)
- Eliminating time-consuming operator intervention, where possible

AUDITING JCL STANDARDS

- Differentiating between test and production jobs
- Specifying naming conventions for JCL parameters (e.g., job names, programmer names, account number formats, and data set names)

The auditor should then determine what procedures are used to enforce compliance with the JCL standards; both manual and automated procedures should be analyzed to determine their strengths and weaknesses. The adequacy of the procedures can be established by performing audit tests of compliance, including:

- Reviewing production JCL for evidence of management review and approval
- Comparing for accuracy current listings of JCL from the production JCL library with that contained in the documentation manual
- Reviewing computer chargeback billing listings for any unidentifiable jobs (e.g., jobs not conforming to the naming conventions)
- Examining the operating system source code and documentation for evidence of JCL editing routines
- Reviewing listings of JCL extracted from the computer's log file (e.g., IBM's SMF file) for evidence of abnormal computer resource utilization (e.g., CPU time, I/O)
- Submitting test JCL for execution to test JCL edit routines

CASE STUDY

The case study described in this chapter involves the specification of IBM operating system (OS) JCL standards, enforcement of the standards through System Management Facility (SMF) exit routines and other procedures, and the audit approach and limitations of auditing JCL standards. This study illustrates how JCL standards were defined and enforced at one installation. The study describes only the major JCL standards and does not present an exhaustive review of IBM OS Job Control Language or JCL standards.

Audit Objectives

The primary criteria for the audit of JCL standards are:
- Adequacy of JCL standards—to ensure that JCL standards prevent computer abuse, support the computer charge-out system, and support naming conventions and documentation standards
- Enforcement of JCL standards—to ensure that procedures exist to prevent, detect, and report the use of nonstandard JCL

Control Standards for JCL

The adequacy of JCL standards must be determined by each installation, depending on applicable control requirements. Although control standards could be applied to all JCL parameters, only the commonly used and important standards are described in this study. These standards are related to the following keyword and positional parameters specified in the job, execute, and data definition JCL statements:

- Job name
- Data set name
- Account numbers
- Programmer's name
- Job class
- Job priority
- Job time and step time limits

Job Name. The job name must contain one through eight alphanumeric and national (#, @, and $) characters; the first character must be alphabetic or national. The job name should be used to identify the application system being tested or in production. The job name may also identify a division within the organization. Some type of identification of the functions of that job should be incorporated in the job name. For example, MPAYSORT would identify a manufacturing job (M) in the payroll system (PAY) that performs a sort (SORT).

Data Set Name. Data sets are specified by the DSNAME or DSN parameter of the DD (data definition) statement. A data set name may contain up to 44 characters, including periods. For each eight or less characters, there must be a period, and the character following the period must be alphabetic or national. Naming conventions for data set names are common in installation JCL standards. It is important that an audit trail be established between the data set name, the job name, the name of the program that creates the data set, and the name of the application system in which the data set belongs. For example, a data set name of MPAY.PAYTRANS.PAY1208.DISK would indicate that the data set is a payroll system file of the manufacturing department (MPAY), is created in job PAYTRANS through the execution of program PAY1208, and resides on magnetic disk storage.

Account Numbers. The account number is a positional parameter coded on the job card. Account numbers are usually established through an internal computer charge-out system.

Generally, account numbers are assigned to each user to identify computer costs to be charged. Regardless of whether the user is a department, a profit center, or a division of the organization, a relationship should exist between the account number and the job name. For example, an account number assigned to the manufacturing department should be used with all jobs involving manufacturing, rather than retailing.

Programmer's Name. The programmer's name parameter, coded on the job card, identifies the person or group responsible for submitting a job. For nonproduction or test jobs, the programmer's name should be coded; for production jobs, the computer scheduler's or operator's name should be coded.

Job Class. The parameter CLASS on the job statement specifies the job class. Job classes can range from A to Z and from 0 to 9, and the installation

AUDITING JCL STANDARDS

must specify which of these 36 possible job classes to use. The computer installation can establish a default class or prevent a job from executing if the job class is omitted.

In determining the classes, installations usually attempt to achieve a balance between I/O- and CPU-bound jobs, between large and small jobs, and so on. Job classes, along with the priority (PRTY) parameter, also determine the overall priority of a job. The operator can start and stop various job classes, thus controlling the time they are run. Jobs in the same job class are grouped together in the input queue to await execution.

Job Priority. The parameter PRTY specifies the priority for selecting jobs from the queue to be executed. The priority may range from 0 (lowest) to 13 (VS1), 14 (in JES3), or 15 (in JES2). If this parameter is not specified on the job statement, the installation may either assign a default priority within the same job class or terminate the job.

Priority is within job class. When several jobs of a given class are awaiting execution, the job with the highest priority within a class is selected first. Jobs with equal priority are selected on a first-in/first-out basis.

Job Time and Step Time Limits. The time parameter sets a CPU time limit for an entire job when it is coded on the job statement. The time parameter may also be coded on the execute statement to set a CPU time limit for a specific step. The two forms of specifying time limits are TIME-minutes and TIME-(minutes, seconds).

Minutes may range from 1 to 1,439 (24 hours); seconds must be less than 60. If the total CPU time for the job exceeds the limit set on the job statement, or if the elapsed CPU time within a step exceeds the time limit for that step, the entire job is abnormally terminated.

Use of the time parameter is good practice; it prevents wasting machine time if the program goes into an endless loop. Because the time parameter is seldom coded in a job, the installation should establish time limits based on the input device. If the job requires more than the established time limit, the specification of the time parameter on the job or execute statement will override that limit.

JCL allows for the coding of TIME-1440; however, this specification will prevent SMF from capturing the CPU time data. The installation can change the limit to prevent this.

Determining the Adequacy of Standards

To determine the adequacy of JCL standards, the auditor must first identify the objectives of the standards (see Table 10-1) and then ascertain whether the standards satisfy the objectives. The standards should support an adequate system of audit trails and controls and should support the objectives of the installation's computer charge-out system.

Table 10-1. Objectives of JCL Standards

Standard	Objective of Standard
Job Name Naming Convention	To identify jobs according to the division of the organization and the computer application system to which they belong
Data Set Naming Convention	To identify the division within the organization and the computer application system to which the data set belongs
	To identify the program that created the data set
	To identify the storage medium of the data set
Account Number	To identify the user department to whom computer charges are billed
Programmer's Name	To identify the programmer or operations scheduler submitting the job
Job Class	To control computer system resources
	To provide for greater system efficiency
Job Priority	To control computer system resources
Job Time and Step Time Limits	To control computer system resources

Audit Trail Objectives. Establishing adequate audit trails is an important objective of JCL standards. Every job submitted to the computer should be traceable to the person who submitted it. Each job should be identified with a particular computer application system or function of the computer installation (e.g., backing up the operating system libraries).

An audit trail should also be established for identifying data sets. As mentioned previously, the data set name should provide information sufficient to identify the storage medium, the program that created the data set, and the application system and division of the user organization in which the data set belongs. In this way, the creation of a data set can be traced to the job that created it and the person who submitted the job.

JCL standards, however, do not prevent a person from submitting an unauthorized job that satisfies the standards. For example, were a programmer to submit a job to create a production data set, he or she would be required to specify, with the same data set name, the job name and program name used to create that production data set. While this unauthorized act cannot be prevented through JCL control standards, it could be detected through the installation's computer charge-out system, by the computer operations department, or by other control procedures described later in this chapter.

Control Objectives. By assigning separate parameter values for job classes, an installation can control the use of core storage, tape drives, disk drives, and other peripherals requested by jobs running in a multiprogramming environment. Within each job class, the installation can designate a job priority value range to provide a mechanism whereby jobs needing quick turnaround will be executed ahead of others. Abuse of the priority system can be controlled by charging higher rates for jobs with higher priorities in the computer charge-out system.

AUDITING JCL STANDARDS

Job time and step time are also controlled by JCL standards. The installation can set time limits for each job entry station to the computer system. Should more time be required, the coding of the TIME parameter on the job or execute statement will override the limit.

Computer Charge-out Billing. The billing system is directly supported by JCL standards. The objective of computer billing is to identify and report charges based on the use of computer resources. This information is captured from each job submitted to the computer and is stored in the SMF files. The account number on the job statement is used to determine who is to be billed for the resources used by that job. Billing statements, which are sent to each user, should include a detailed listing of each job submitted to the computer. The listing should contain the job name, programmer name, account number, job class, and job priority, in addition to the charges for the job. Subtotals can be provided by job name or programmer name on the report. Without JCL standards, the detailed billing reports would contain unidentifiable jobs submitted by unidentifiable persons.

Enforcement of JCL Standards

The most effective method of enforcing JCL standards is through the coding of SMF exit routines; this coding prevents the use of nonstandard JCL. SMF exits are installation-written routines linked to the SMF control program for monitoring jobs or job steps at various points in their processing cycle. An installation may insert code in any or all of the SMF exits to prevent a job that does not conform to installation standards from executing. SMF will automatically provide dummy routines for all unused exits.

SMF supplies a number of exits that can be linked to the user-written exit routines. These exit routines include:
- Input stream validation exit (IEFUIV [OS/VS1 only])
- Job validation exit (IEFUJV)
- Job initiation exit (IEFUJI)
- Step initiation exit (IEFUSI)
- Time limit exit (IEFUTL)
- SYSOUT limit exit (IEFUSO)
- SMF record exit (IEFU83)
- Termination exit (IEFACTRT)
- Job purge exit (IEFUJP)
- SMF dump exit (IEFU29 [OS/VS2 MVS only])

In addition to the coding of SMF exit routines, a partitioned data set (PDS) must also be created to store the authorized parameter values. This includes values for the job names, account numbers, programmers' names, application system names, job classes, and job priorities. The card image records located in each PDS are converted into an assembler program, which is then assembled into an object program. The SMF exit routine calls in the object program as a subroutine at the time a job is submitted. The SMF exit routines pass the parameter values located in the job to the authorized values in the appropriate subroutines. (The technique of using a subroutine instead of reading the values from a PDS saves CPU time and eliminates I/O.) Parameter values that are not authorized are identified as invalid, and the job is abnormally terminated.

Auditing Enforcement Standards

The objective of auditing JCL enforcement controls is to determine whether these controls effectively prevent the use of nonstandard JCL. To satisfy this objective, the auditor should review the controls for authorization, SMF exit program testing, and backup.

Authorization Controls. Management must authorize the parameter values to be used in JCL. These authorizations can originate from several sources but must be made in writing in order to provide an adequate audit trail. The programming manager and operations manager should be responsible for submitting documentation to the systems software department, authorizing adds, changes, and deletes to the programmer's name parameter file. For example, written authorization for changes to the account number parameter should come from the person in charge of computer billing. Management must also authorize changes to the assigned values that identify the application system and the division of the organization, which together specify the job name parameter values. The auditor should review these written authorizations to the parameter values stored in the PDSs for accuracy.

The auditor should also be satisfied that JCL standards are adequately described in the installation's documentation standards manual. This manual represents a clear statement of management's authorization of all JCL standards.

Program Testing Controls. The effectiveness of enforcing JCL standards is determined by the ability of the SMF exit routines to successfully identify nonstandard JCL. The auditor may conduct a detailed code review of each exit program to determine if the coding is accurate; however, because the coding is somewhat complex, a more effective audit approach would involve submitting test data to the programs. Two methods of testing can be used.

The auditor can submit nonstandard JCL parameter values to the system through manually prepared JCL run decks to test the SMF exit programs. To fully test the programs, the auditor should include symbolic parameters and cataloged JCL parameters in the testing. The exit routines should reject all nonstandard JCL parameters and ABEND the job.

The second and more effective means of testing is the use of IBM's TESTEXIT procedure. This procedure involves an assembler language source program (also named TESTEXIT) that attaches a data generator utility program (IEBDG) to create sample parameter lists. The source program then calls each SMF exit routine being tested and passes the appropriate parameter list to it. Figure 10-1 illustrates the I/O and control flow of the TESTEXIT

AUDITING JCL STANDARDS

Figure 10-1. TESTEXIT I/O and Control Flow

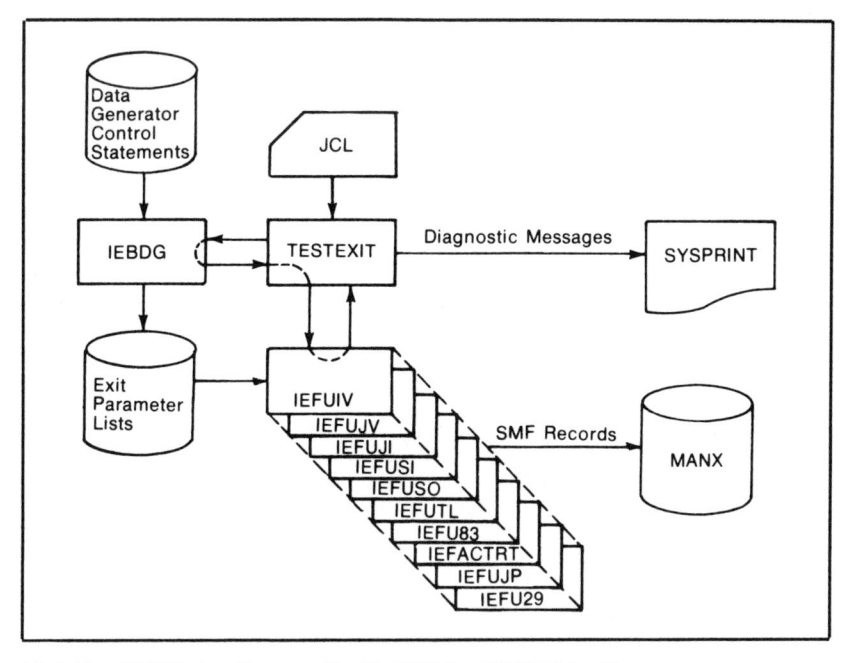

Adapted from OS/VS1 Systems Management Facilities (SMF), Form GC24-5115-2, p. 60

source program. As with the manually prepared JCL parameters submitted in the first approach, all nonstandard JCL parameter values should be rejected.

Backup Controls. Adequate backup procedures are of critical importance in an installation that enforces JCL standards through the use of SMF exit programs. For example, it is possible to introduce program errors into an SMF exit program that would prevent any job from being executed by the operating system, including a job that would attempt to correct the errors. Because of this risk, it is necessary to copy the operating system libraries prior to the loading of an updated version of the SMF exit programs. This backup copy can then be used as input for a standalone program (a program that can be executed without the need of the operating system) to write over the current operating system libraries containing the SMF exit program errors. The system can then be brought back up with an IPL. It is imperative that the auditor review backup controls that provide adequate system recovery.

Audit Reliance on JCL Standards

The auditor can use information generated from JCL for auditing the computer charge-out billing system and computer application systems in the IBM OS environment. Reliance on JCL standards, therefore, is of critical importance in performing compliance and substantive audit tests of the data generated by computer jobs.

Several audit tests can be performed. For example, the auditor can use the SMF files storing the data to extract all jobs run for an application system by employing the naming convention standard of the job name. In addition, the auditor can extract and print a list of all data sets of an application system by using the naming convention standards of the data set name. The auditor would be able to test for compliance to naming convention standards and to determine whether individuals (as indicated by the programmer's name parameter) were authorized to execute certain jobs and create particular data sets.

As mentioned previously, the enforcement of JCL standards through user-written SMF exit routines does not prevent a programmer from submitting a job that masquerades as a production job or that identifies some other programmer as the one who submitted the job. Unauthorized activity of this type may be detected by management review of daily SMF reports listing all jobs submitted. While this procedure does not guarantee detection, it does serve as a deterrent to those contemplating an unauthorized act. If this procedure does not exist, the auditor should recommend that a management review policy be adopted.

CONCLUSION

JCL standards are an important and powerful management tool for identifying computer job audit trails and controls. The use of standards supports management's control over computer information processing. Because JCL standards have a substantial impact on documentation standards, computer charge-out billing, the control of computer resources, and computer job audit trails, the EDP auditor must be concerned with the adequacy and enforcement of these standards. The auditor must also rely on computer job information when performing audits of the computer charge-out billing system and computer application system audits.

Bibliography

Brown, G.D. *System/370 Job Control Language*. New York: John Wiley & Sons, 1977.

Data Processing Division, IBM Corp. *OS/VS1 JCL Reference*. Form GC24-5099-3. White Plains, NY: IBM, 1976.

Data Processing Division, IBM Corp. *OS/VS1 JCL Services*. Form GC24-5100-1. White Plains, NY: IBM, 1975.

Data Processing Division, IBM Corp. *OS/VS1 Systems Management Facilities (SMF)*. Form GC24-5115-2. White Plains, NY: IBM, 1978.

Dolotta, T.A. "Command and Job Control Languages." *Encyclopedia of Computer Science*. Edited by A. Ralston. New York: Van Nostrand Reinhold Co, 1976.

Jardine, D.A. "The Structure of Operating System Control Languages." *Command Languages*. Edited by C. Unger. Amsterdam: North Holland; New York: American Elsevier, 1975.

11 Auditing Minicomputer-Based Systems

by Thomas H. Fitzgerald

INTRODUCTION

Minicomputers, which perform various tasks in the modern DP environment, can be used as anything from standalone processors to satellite WP stations. The term "minicomputer," however, is actually a misnomer because its hardware capabilities are often greater than those of the mainframes and maxicomputers used in the early 1970s.

What, then, makes a minicomputer a minicomputer? The answer is nebulous at times. A minicomputer is often defined as a computer system designed to be operated by a small staff in the end-user's environment and used to process one specific application, as opposed to multiple concurrent applications. The applications processed vary from simple batch data collection to online, real-time applications.

EDP auditors frequently encounter minicomputers that are used as the main processor for applications that have direct bearing on corporate financial statements. Although traditional control and audit objectives can be applied to such systems, the auditor must be aware of the unique hardware features and special exposures presented by minicomputers.

He must also realize that an organization chooses to install minicomputers because they are cost-effective; as a result, many traditional audit and control mechanisms may not always be cost-justifiable. The auditor must then be prepared to accept alternate control techniques, even though they often do not provide the same level of protection as do traditional controls. This chapter discusses common audit and control problems presented by minicomputer systems and suggests alternate techniques to achieve audit and control objectives.

TYPES OF MINICOMPUTERS

Intelligent Terminals

Depending on the complexity of the application, intelligent terminals can be either mini- or microcomputers. Basically, these devices edit and validate input data prior to entering the data into the master files. Driven by a host processor, these terminals usually contain sufficient intelligence to perform simple tasks at the terminal. The intelligence can be in the form of computer programs, which can be modified by the user, or PROM (Programmable Read Only Memory), which is supplied by the hardware manufacturer.

The applications usually check data input for proper format and may even verify certain key data elements for accuracy. When the system stores data and then forwards it to a remote processor after normal hours, the terminal acts as a data gatherer and, to some extent, verifies the data input. At a certain time of day, all information stored is transmitted to a host processor for update to the master files.

An intelligent terminal system is also responsible for terminal and operator security, ensuring that the data has been entered by an authorized user. The auditor should review the procedures for issuing system passwords, terminal transaction capabilities, error detection, and follow-up of security violations. For store-and-forward systems, the auditor can verify the accuracy of processing over key data elements and determine the processing timing between the terminal and the host computer. The auditor should be concerned with backup of data storage and should evaluate the risk of data loss as well as the potential impact such a loss could have on the processing cycle.

Remote Job Entry (RJE) Systems

RJE systems usually are found only in large DP installations where the central computer is removed from the DP development sites. The DP development group uses the system to enter test runs against the system. Basically, the system is a remote card reader used to enter computer jobs into the central site computer. The user is responsible for initiating batch programs to be executed at the central site.

The auditor should ensure that the central computer's operating system software controls the types of jobs that can be initiated from an RJE station. Under no circumstances should production data sets be accessible through an RJE station. If the operating system does not allow specific deterrent controls to be implemented centrally, the RJE site must be subject to the same access and security controls as is the central site computer.

The auditor should treat this system as a direct card reader that can bypass the control mechanisms set up in the data or job control areas of the central site computer.

Communications Processors (Front-End Minis)

The communications processor is one of the most common types of minicomputer installation. Basically, the minicomputer is located between the central system and the communications system user. The minicomputer is responsible for line protocols and polling sequences, line security, message restart and recovery, store-and-forward operations, and message delivery.

AUDITING MINICOMPUTER-BASED SYSTEMS

Before allowing access to the main computer, the minicomputer requires terminal authentication and operator verification. In larger installations, some of the central site functions (e.g., security) are down-loaded to a communications minicomputer.

The auditor's primary concerns with front-end minicomputers are the terminal security features and the manual procedures covering follow-up of security violations. The level of line security necessary depends on the importance of the message traffic on the system. The auditor should ensure that data encryption techniques are used when compromise of message traffic represents a risk of substantial financial loss.

In addition, the auditor should evaluate the effectiveness and efficiency of the controls over the acquisition and maintenance of the minicomputer's software.

Standalone Processors

The remainder of this chapter discusses the unique problems caused by minicomputers used as standalone processors. The most common internal control weakness found in a small installation with a standalone minicomputer is a lack of adequate separation of duties. Typically, only one operator runs the computer facility and, by simply turning on the system, can affect all data loaded and possibly even modify the software to perpetrate fraud. Although this concentration of duties in one operator presents an unacceptable exposure, the cost of hiring another operator is usually prohibitive.

In evaluating such an installation, the auditor must recognize that the cost of implementing certain controls must not outweigh the benefits to be derived from their use. Although an ideal separation of duties is often impossible to achieve in a standalone minicomputer environment, the auditor can suggest the control techniques discussed in the next section to offset the weakness without dramatically increasing operating cost.

CONTROL TECHNIQUES IN MINICOMPUTER SYSTEMS

The primary control objective in a minicomputer environment is ensuring that complete, authorized, and accurate information is processed according to system design. The auditor should evaluate the following control techniques to determine whether they can achieve the objectives established for the particular environment being examined.

Figure 11-1 is an audit questionnaire that can be used to determine whether the following control techniques are established and used.

Rotation of Duties

Because a minimal amount of specialized training is needed to operate a minicomputer, the organization should train more than one individual to run the computer. By rotating duties regularly (from data entry to operator to

Questions	Response Yes	No	NA	Comments
A. Rotation of Duties				
1. Is more than one person trained to operate the computer?				
2. Are job functions rotated regularly?				
3. Is a separate person responsible for software maintenance?				
4. Are functions clearly documented?				
5. Do checks and balances exist where concentration of duties is minimized?				
B. Increased User Participation				
1. Is the user involved in the proof function associated with the system?				
2. Has the responsibility for proof and control been concentrated where there is now a weakness?				
3. Are proof and control functions reasonably separated?				
C. Increased Management Participation				
1. Is a log of jobs run maintained?				
2. Is this log reviewed and approved by appropriate management?				
3. Is the user aware of the jobs attributed to him?				
4. Is all time accounted for and gaps reconciled?				
D. Restricted Access to Input Terminals				
1. Do passwords or physical security features exist for terminals?				
2. Are controls over passwords or keys appropriate for the application system?				
E. Follow-up on Security Violations				
1. Does the application system recognize and report unauthorized access attempts to appropriate management?				
2. Do formal instructions cover security violations?				
3. Is management aware of the actions to be taken following an access violation?				
F. Program Library and Data Storage Controls				
1. Are all changes to applications software logged?				
2. Is access to applications software libraries restricted?				
3. Are all changes to the application documented?				
4. Can the computer operator change the application code without assistance?				

Figure 11-1. Internal Control Questionnaire

AUDITING MINICOMPUTER-BASED SYSTEMS

	Response	
Questions	Yes | No | NA	Comments

G. Controls over Powerful Utilities
  1. Are controls adequate to ensure management involvement when system utilities are executed?
  2. Are the uses of these modules logged?

H. Preformatted Input Screens
  1. Does the application use transaction-oriented screens?
  2. Does the applications software contain sufficient edits?

I. Batch Totals by Input Device
  1. Has the system been designed to facilitate proof and control of data entered?
  2. Do automated proof procedures exist, and are manual procedures adequate to research differences?

J. Verification of Input
  1. Are proof controls over data entered appropriate?
  2. Does the system provide verification of input?
  3. Are the procedures for error correction accurate?
  4. Does the system capture the identification of the operator entering or correcting the data?

K. Proof and Control Function
  1. Is the proof and control function sufficient to detect errors and omissions in a timely fashion?
  2. Is the control function independent of the user?

L. Turnkey System Control
  1. Are the controls associated with the system sufficient to protect the firm from risk of loss?
  2. Can the system be maintained by in-house personnel if necessary?
  3. Has the vendor provided all needed documentation?
  4. Is the documentation sufficient to maintain and operate the system?

M. Backup and Recovery
  1. Has an alternate site with compatible equipment been located?
  2. Has this site been tested?
  3. Does a batch entry facility exist for online systems?
  4. Does software exist to back up and restore master files?

Figure 11-1. (Cont)

Questions	Response			Comments
	Yes	No	NA	
N. Physical Security				
1. Are access control mechanisms appropriate to the application?				
2. Are logs of visitors maintained by the area?				
O. Logical Security				
1. Are passwords changed regularly?				
2. Is the procedure for entering new users on the system adequate?				
3. Does a procedure exist to delete users from the system in a timely manner?				
P. Data Security				
1. Has a risk assessment of data security requirements been completed?				
2 Does an appropriate data security strategy exist?				
Q. In-House Development Controls				
1. Does a vehicle exist to evaluate the importance of a system being developed for a minicomputer?				
2. If differences in development controls are allowed, are the reasons documented?				
3. Does a separate set of development standards exist for a minicomputer? If so, are they adequate?				
R. Existing System Modifications				
1. Are changes to applications software reviewed by management?				
2. Are responsibilities for maintenance rotated among all programming personnel?				
3. Are changes communicated to the user prior to going live?				
4. Does the user prepare an acceptance test of changes?				
5. Are programmers prohibited from updating program libraries?				
6. Are all changes made in source form, and are they documented?				

Figure 11-1. (Cont)

proof clerk), the organization can prevent fraudulent manipulation of data. Furthermore, if additional personnel are trained to operate the system, the problems encountered during vacations or illness are alleviated.

Increased User Participation

When specific user personnel are responsible for the system in general, they can be assigned the task of verifying and controlling data. This alternative must be evaluated carefully, however, since its use can compromise accounting controls. For example, if this option is used indiscriminately, too many functions can be concentrated in the user area.

The auditor should prepare control flowcharts of the user area and the computer system to pinpoint existing controls and to determine whether the controls are concentrated in the user area and whether separation can be achieved at a reasonable cost.

If separation cannot be achieved without a significant cost increase, the auditor should suggest alternate control techniques. On the other hand, if the risks associated with the system are great, the organization should consider absorbing the increased operating costs.

Increased Management Participation

The minicomputer can usually produce a console log of all jobs processed. The equipment contains a start/stop clock that indicates the amount of computer time used. Management should require and review a manual log of all jobs run, with start and stop times, to ensure that all time is accounted for and all jobs run were authorized. Ideally, the computer should produce a machine listing of jobs run to be distributed to user personnel for verification.

Restricted Access to Input Terminals

Depending on the sophistication of the application, online terminals associated with the minicomputer can be subject to standard controls, including passwords and terminal identification procedures. As an alternative to passwords, management can physically lock the terminals and institute controls over the keys. User management should be responsible for the controls over the keys and for changing the passwords periodically.

Follow-up on Security Violations

User management should be required to institute procedures to investigate security violations and unauthorized attempts to access the computer through an input terminal. The computer application system should have mechanisms that prevent unauthorized access to the system and that report security violations to appropriate user management for follow-up.

Program Library and Data Storage Controls

The typical minicomputer installation does not justify a full-time librarian. This function can be performed by a person other than the computer operator, who should never be permitted sole access to master files and program libraries. The data control person who reconciles output can be assigned responsibility for the program library, and the function can be rotated regularly.

A key element of control is the integrity of the applications software library. While controls over changes to applications software are never foolproof, the auditor can easily detect unauthorized changes by establishing audit trails.

Controls over Powerful Utilities

The minicomputer environment is unique in that it has vendor-supplied utility programs that can modify data or application programs through console messages or control cards. Although these programs are necessary, they increase the risk of exposure to unauthorized use and data manipulation. Therefore, controls over these programs are especially significant to data integrity and system security.

Passwords that are controlled by user management should be used to access these programs. User management, however, should not be able to operate the computer without assistance. In installations where this technique is not feasible, these utilities should be removed from the system and placed under the control of user management in load or object form.

The auditor must ensure that these utilities cannot be executed by one person and that management involvement is required to execute these programs.

Preformatted Input Screens

An effective control technique for online applications is the use of full, preformatted screens to ensure that all data entered into the system is complete. If a terminal operator does not enter all necessary data, the system will reject the transaction. The application software also performs edits and checks to ensure that all information entered is in the proper format. The use of preformatted screens ensures that only transaction-oriented data can be entered by the terminal operator.

Batch Totals by Input Device

The computer application software should be designed to provide record counts, batch totals, and dollar control figures by each input station or operator. Management should require detailed proof and control procedures by input station.

As an alternate control, the terminal operator should be required to enter a batch total and item count that can be reconciled with the totals the system accumulates. If there is a discrepancy between totals, an area supervisor should determine the cause of the error and make an appropriate correction.

Verification of Input

For batch data collection systems, input data, or at least key data elements, should be verified. These systems usually replace keypunch areas, and input source documents are entered through terminals and forwarded to a host processor after all data has been entered. This type of processor system should require verification and batch totals by input station.

The system should be designed with controls that ensure that all data has been entered correctly. The proof function provided by the software should be sufficiently sophisticated to provide automated reconcilements and a facility for supervisor override of corrections.

Proof and Control Function

The application system should provide a method for reconciling data entered and sufficient clerical procedures for recognizing and correcting errors. Internally generated entries should be provided, and total changes should be reconciled with master file balances and record counts to guard against errors and omissions.

Summary of Transactions Entered

The application system should produce a detailed listing of all transactions entered to provide an audit trail. This listing should contain the source of the data entered (operator ID and terminal number), a reconcilement by data station, and a total system reconcilement.

Turnkey System Controls

When the auditor is faced with a system purchased or supplied by a hardware vendor or consulting firm, he usually has little control over the design alternatives built into the system. He must still evaluate, however, the overall control methodologies and report on their adequacy.

In addition, the auditor must ensure that documentation standards are adhered to and that the vendor provides sufficient documentation to allow maintenance of the package, including source code (to protect the firm in case of the demise of the vendor), program specifications, design descriptions, and complete file layouts. He should also see that the vendor provides complete operating instructions and training.

Backup and Recovery

Backup and recovery procedures for standalone minicomputers are similar to those needed in large mainframe environments. The system must produce a log file containing before and after image records and provide utility programs for backing up and reloading data sets. The problem with the minicomputer is that most backup and recovery functions are not part of the system operating software but are user-generated code. Thus, the auditor must ensure that this code has been generated and can provide sufficient backup and recovery control.

Another problem in a minicomputer environment is locating an alternate processing site in case of emergency. The hardware vendor can usually facilitate backup site arrangements. The auditor, however, should ensure that the alternate site is compatible and tested periodically. For online systems, a batch data entry facility should be available to allow data to be entered without using an online terminal.

The auditor must ensure that sufficient backup and recovery strategies exist because the end user generally selects a minicomputer system without realizing the importance of backup, and he cannot rely on DP to supply this backup.

Physical Security

Many minicomputers are designed to operate within the user's environment without special site requirements; consequently, the computer is often installed in such a manner that applying physical security is almost impossible. In addition, the cost of installing access-restricting devices is prohibitive. A risk analysis should be performed to determine the degree of risk that could occur should site security be compromised.

In some cases, access restrictions on the user area are sufficient to prevent unauthorized personnel from obtaining access to the hardware. These procedures involve badges or keylock systems. In critical applications, management may be able to cost-justify keeping the operations staff both physically separate and visible at all times.

Logical Security

The application system should be designed to allow only authorized personnel to use the system. In an online environment, this requires positive identification of the terminal user by keylock or password. The system should also include an automatic log-off capability on terminals that have been inactive for a predetermined period of time.

Password change is generally the user's responsibility. The auditor should ensure that passwords are changed periodically and that procedures exist for recognizing and approving new users and for deleting users.

Data Security

One of the most difficult objectives to accomplish in a minicomputer environment is effective data security. Because the availability of software packages that protect data on minicomputers is generally nonexistent, software should be developed in-house to restrict and control access to sensitive information.

The user of the system must determine the risks associated with the information stored on the system and have the auditor review that assessment.

Because this assessment is generally subjective, the auditor must also ensure that management has an objective view of the risks involved and that its decisions are based on accurate information.

In-House Development Controls

Controls over new application systems must be evaluated based on the importance of the system. In-house development of critical application systems must be subject to the same controls as those applied to the development of large-scale systems, including complete system documentation, user manuals, and user training.

Existing System Modifications

Because the minicomputer staff is usually small, application system maintenance is a problem. For example, controls over changes to application systems are often lax. The person who developed the system is usually assigned to the maintenance function, and review of change by a quality assurance group is often missing, leaving the maintenance programmer's actions uncontrolled.

The auditor, therefore, must ensure that the maintenance function is controlled, that change procedures are standardized, and that at least two persons are required in order to change the program library. In addition, the auditor should ensure that the following controls are in place:

- Changes are made in source-code form.
- Changes are authorized and reviewed by management.
- The programmers involved update the existing documentation to reflect the change.
- The change is communicated to the user.
- The user tests the change.
- Access to the production source and load libraries is strictly controlled.
- Maintenance responsibilities are rotated when possible.
- If the programmer requires hands-on test access to the system, live data files are not to reside on the system.
- Programs are not changed in load or object form.

CONCLUSION

The auditor can use risk analysis techniques to evaluate the importance of the applications processed on the minicomputer. If a critical application is running on a minicomputer, the auditor must apply the same level of control as that found in a large-scale computer environment.

Although the minicomputer poses unique control problems, management must realize that today's minicomputers are as sophisticated as the mainframe computers of several years ago and, therefore, require protection against deliberate or accidental modification or loss of data.

12 Hardware Acquisition Cost/Benefit Review

by Bryan Wilkinson

INTRODUCTION

In the early days of automation, companies acquired computers to keep up with the competition—never mind how or whether the equipment would be used. A story is told of a DP manager whose replacement entered a room and found it full of gear that had never been hooked up. A medical facility in the Midwest had an IBM 360/155 that they were planning to upgrade, although the only application being run was payroll. To protect the foolish, the companies shall remain nameless.

Fortunately, the mystique surrounding computers and DP is vanishing. Management has come to realize that a computer is just another tool, like a drill press or an X-ray scanner. As a result, many companies are beginning to require that the acquisition or upgrading of equipment be justified, just as with any other expensive hardware. Before approval is given to buy or lease computer equipment, knowledgeable executives should know:

- What it will cost to acquire and install
- What it will cost to operate
- When it will be fully operational
- What measurable benefits will result
- What nonquantifiable benefits can be expected
- What operations will be affected by the change
- What the effect will be if schedules are not met
- What controls will be in place to monitor progress and to ensure that the project is successfully completed

Assuming the answers are satisfactory, the project can be approved, and acquisition and implementation can begin.

Sometime after the project is completed, management (or the auditor in his role as monitor of company assets) should ask whether events happened as they were supposed to:

- Were expenditures within the limits established?
- Were the promised benefits achieved?
- Was the impact no worse than forecasted?
- Is the equipment working "as advertised?"
- Were the schedules met?

If the answer to any of these questions is no, the reason should be documented, as should the steps that can be taken to prevent such results in the future. EDP auditors are equipped to find the answers to these questions and should conduct post-installation audits of major hardware acquisition projects as a matter of course. Note that the analyses of costs and anticipated benefits described in this chapter can also be used in contract negotiations.

INITIATING THE AUDIT

Not every hardware project should be audited. Company management, audit management, or perhaps the EDP auditor should establish an expenditures minimum below which audits are not made. This minimum will vary from company to company, based most likely on prior successes or failures in equipment acquisitions—the more successes, the higher the limit. As with any company activity, there should be the potential for a favorable pay-back from the post-installation audit.

Because planned acquisition and installation costs are a major consideration in deciding which audits to perform, the EDP auditor should be aware of approved hardware acquisitions. If the company does not have a formal approval procedure, the auditor should keep a list of all hardware additions and changes.

It is important that the auditor be aware of *all* equipment changes, not just those above the minimum cost. The reason for this is that some DP managers use a nickle-and-dime approach to hardware acquisitions. They acquire a CRT here, a disk drive there. The result is that no single acquisition is large enough to cause much notice or, perhaps, even to require justification. When all expenditures are added together, however, the outlay may be substantial. Situations like this require special handling and have some management implications. Either the DP manager is trying to beat the system of approvals (a clear warning signal), or he or she is unable to properly forecast his requirements (a warning signal of a different type).

Besides determining which projects to audit, the auditor must determine when to conduct the audit. A true post-installation audit should be conducted after all costs have been incurred and after enough time has elapsed for most of the planned benefits and objectives to have been achieved. It should not be conducted so late, however, that relevant documentation has been destroyed or undocumented occurrences forgotten by the participants. Experienced auditors generally try to conduct post-installation audits from three to six months after the project is completed. With such a timetable, however, the auditor may be told that insufficient time has elapsed to achieve the promised benefits; the accuracy of such protestations should be evaluated.

The auditor may be confronted with a project of extremely long duration (e.g., more than five years). In such a situation, it is often advisable to conduct a post-installation audit while the project is still going on. In addition to the audit questions listed earlier, the following questions should be answered:

HARDWARE COST/BENEFIT REVIEW

- Should the project have been broken up, and should it now be broken into several projects of limited scope and duration?
- Is progress to date, both with regard to costs and benefits, according to plan?
- What are the prospects of staying within budget?
- What are the prospects of achieving the planned goals and objectives?
- Are there project controls not in place that should be implemented?
- Are the existing project controls working well?
- Are there steps that should be taken to expedite project completion?
- Would it be advisable to terminate the project at this point?

Planning Documentation Review

After choosing the project to be reviewed, the auditor should obtain all relevant planning (feasibility) studies. The forms and documents prepared for a formal request procedure (if there is one) should also be obtained. If the project plans were revised after the project was started, these revisions, whether or not formally approved by management, should be obtained.

The costs, benefits, and schedules in these planning documents represent the commitments or plans for the project. The auditor should compare these plans with the actual expenditures and accomplishments. The causes of significant variance should, as much as possible, be determined.

The planning documents should be reviewed carefully by an experienced EDP auditor, noting data that will be pulled off for audit schedules. During the first review, it is useful to highlight the installation costs, operation costs, quantified benefits, and nonquantified benefits with different colors. These highlighted documents go into the working papers as backup for the audit schedules.

Audit Schedules

Various costs and anticipated benefits (see Table 12-1) should be shown on four audit schedules:
- Installation Costs Schedule
- Operation Costs Schedule
- Quantified Benefits Schedule
- Nonquantified Benefits Schedule

Installation Costs Schedule. The Installation Costs Schedule should consist of the planned, *onetime costs* associated with acquiring and installing the equipment. These should be shown by type or source of cost. If these costs are to be incurred over a period of time, the planned expenditures should be shown by time period (e.g., month, quarter, or year). Because slipped schedules can affect installation costs, the scheduled dates for implementation and other milestones should be recorded. If there are revised plans and costs, the revised data should be placed on the schedule, preferably in columns adjacent to the original figures. This gives the auditor an overview of the changes that

Table 12-1. Types of Costs and Benefits to be Reviewed

A. **Installation Costs**
   Facilities costs
   Hardware and communications costs
   Support equipment costs
   Cost of start-up supplies
   Miscellaneous costs
   One-time personnel costs
B. **Operation Costs**
   Facilities costs
   Hardware and communications costs
   Cost of supplies
   Miscellaneous costs
   Personnel costs
C. **Quantified Benefits**
   Monetary savings
   Nonmonetary savings
D. **Nonquantified Benefits**

---

have occurred during the life of the project. Significant changes should be questioned if the documentation contains no explanation.

Operation Costs Schedule. The Operation Costs Schedule should contain the planned, *recurring costs* associated with acquiring and installing the equipment. In all probability the auditor will want to record these costs on a monthly basis; annual property tax, for example, would be divided by 12 to arrive at a monthly figure. Again, if revised plans contain estimates of operation costs, the various estimates should be entered on the schedule and significant variations questioned.

Quantified Benefits Schedule. The Quantified Benefits Schedule should contain the planned benefits to which a numerical value has been assigned. Items involving dollar savings can be grouped together, followed by items to which a dollar value has not been assigned. In some instances, a quantity that is not in the plan can readily be obtained by the auditor. For example, the proposal might say that the new equipment will increase the number of transactions handled per operator by 25 percent. If the number of transactions handled when the proposal was prepared is available, the auditor can easily compute the transactions-per-employee target. As such, this benefit could appear on this schedule; however, if data on transactions-per-employee is not available, this benefit should be placed in the Nonquantified Benefits Schedule because there is no way to quantitatively determine whether or not it has been realized. As before, where revised plans exist, changes in planned benefits should be recorded.

Nonquantified Benefits Schedule. The Nonquantified Benefits Schedule should contain all benefits to which numerical values cannot be assigned. These benefits tend to be scattered throughout the proposal to make it sound good and to make it more salable (e.g., "improved company image," "improved morale," "reports that are easier to use," "more accuracy").

HARDWARE COST/BENEFIT REVIEW

The plans and proposals must be carefully reviewed to detect all such items. Because these phrases may do more to sell the proposal than do any quantified benefits, they must be evaluated in a post-installation audit. The auditor should expect to see changes in these benefits from one revision of a plan to the next because they do not represent changes in goals but, rather, changes in writing styles. This being the case, all such benefits, regardless of which version of a plan or proposal they appear in, should be candidates for evaluation.

When preparing these four schedules, the auditor should leave room to record the actual figures. If the plan calls for costs or benefits by time period, the actual figures should be recorded for the same time periods. If schedules have slipped, the actual figures will be recorded over more periods than the plan calls for. The auditor should, therefore, leave space on each schedule for costs and benefits not anticipated in the plan.

INSTALLATION COSTS

Installation costs are one-time costs associated with installing computers and computer-related equipment. Some of these costs can be expensed and thus properly belong on the Installation Costs Schedule; others can be capitalized. The auditor must determine whether to show capitalized costs on the Installation Costs Schedule, as the Operation Costs Schedule calls for depreciation or amortization costs. The Installation Costs Schedule will reflect all one-time outlays if capitalized costs are included. Caution must be used in any presentation combining installation and operation costs, however, because capitalized costs will be expensed over the useful life of the equipment.

The one-time costs associated with installing computers and computer-related equipment can be grouped into the following areas:
- Facility costs
- Hardware and communications costs
- Support equipment costs
- Start-up supplies and miscellaneous costs
- One-time personnel costs

In the following breakdown of these types of costs, note that not all costs apply to every equipment project. Some costs not included in this checklist may also be encountered and should be included on the schedule.

Facilities Costs

If this is an audit of the first computer installation, there will be some facilities costs; if this is an audit of an equipment change or addition, there may also be facilities costs. Types of facilities costs are:
- Building purchase(s)—This includes down payments, points, commissions, finders fees, inspection fees, and permits.
- Building construction and/or building or leasehold remodeling or improvement—This includes one-time labor and materials costs for installing and moving walls, permanent shelving, roofing, and other

improvements not covered elsewhere.
- Raised floor—This includes materials and installation.
- Power and electrical—This includes labor and materials for transformers, wiring, fixtures, cabling, and emergency power-off switches.
- Plumbing—This covers the plumbing for water-cooled computers. Additional plumbing for employee needs would be listed as a building or leasehold improvement cost.
- Air conditioning for the computer equipment.
- Fire-control systems—This includes the purchase and installation costs of detectors, alarms, sprinkler systems, fire-retardant systems, and smoke/exhaust systems.
- Security systems—This includes the purchase and installation costs of unauthorized-entry detectors and alarms, key-card systems, combination-lock entry systems, and window bars.

Hardware and Communications Costs

Because computers, computer-related equipment, and communications technology are changing so fast, many companies lease or rent, rather than buy, their equipment. Lease or rental costs would appear on the Operation Costs Schedule. One-time equipment-related costs include the following:
- Computer mainframe—When recording actual costs, the gross and net purchase price should be recorded. Net is calculated as gross minus any recovery from sale or trade-in of an existing mainframe.
- Peripherals—It may be desirable to list separately such items as tape drives, disk drives, card readers, and card punches. Gross and net cost, if any, should be recorded.
- Remote terminals—This includes printers, CRTs, keyboard devices, and RJE equipment. Gross and net cost, if any, should be recorded.
- Communications equipment—This includes data phones, modems, multiplexors, concentrators, front-end computers, and microwave systems. Gross and net cost, if any, should be recorded.
- Data entry equipment—This includes keypunch machines, verifiers, key-to-tape systems, key-to-disk systems, and key-to-diskette systems. Gross and net costs, if any, should be recorded.
- Buy-out costs of any existing leases.
- Ship-out costs of old equipment, including crating, drayage, and freight.
- Hookup costs.
- Purchase price of any software (e.g., operating system) required for the equipment.

Any sales tax paid should be listed.

Support Equipment

Support equipment costs tend to be overlooked, particularly by the first-time computer user. They include:
- EAM (i.e., card) equipment (which is becoming increasingly less common)

HARDWARE COST/BENEFIT REVIEW

- Output-related support equipment, including bursters, decollaters, continuous-forms check signers, auxiliary reproducers that handle continuous-forms output (i.e., those not connected to the computer)
- Carts, dollies, cabinets, shelves, tables, chairs, and miscellaneous furniture
- Fire extinguishers, floor pullers, and other miscellaneous equipment

Start-up Supplies and Miscellaneous Costs

Although supplies are usually thought of as an operating expense, there can be one-time costs for them. There are also miscellaneous costs connected with installing a computer for the first time or making an equipment change. These include:
- The first group of tapes, disks, and diskettes (i.e., those purchased to get the system going)
- The cost of scrapping punch cards and other forms and supplies that are incompatible with the new equipment (e.g., a change in disk drives that obsoletes disk packs)
- File conversions associated with the equipment change (but not those associated with system changes)
- Program changes and reprogramming associated with the equipment change (but not those associated with system changes)

One-Time Personnel Costs

There are a few one-time personnel costs that should not be neglected:
- Recruiting costs, including advertising and travel of applicants
- Hiring costs, including agency fees and relocation expense
- Training people to use the new equipment, including tuition, travel, purchase of training materials, and salaries and benefits while training
- Consultant fees and expenses incurred to assist in the equipment conversion

Effect of Time on Costs

Given the current state of the economy and the volatility of computer capability and prices, elapsed time between approval of a proposal and its implementation can cause a significant difference between planned and actual costs.

In one case, the price of a mainframe dropped drastically between the date of approval to purchase and the actual purchase, but all other expenses associated with the equipment change were higher than planned. Because of the mainframe's drop in price (which came about because the vendor announced a new series of computers), the project came in under budget. Looking at the total dollars spent, it appeared that the manager was doing a good job. He may have been, but maybe he was just lucky.

In another case, the purchase of 20 CRTs was authorized. Then a new terminal that performed about comparably and sold for less than half the cost was announced. Consequently, 45 terminals were purchased instead of 20 since the "total cost was the same"; no study was made to see whether 45 terminals were needed. In fact, when the audit was done, they were being underutilized. The auditor pointed out that management had authorized the acquisition of 20 terminals, not the spending of X dollars.

Unfortunately, the passage of time does not always result in lower costs—quite the contrary. Because of inflation, many costs, particularly labor, escalate if schedules are slipped. For this reason, the auditor should note the date when expenditures were planned and compare it with the date they were actually made. If schedule slippages adversely affect costs, as is generally the case, the auditor will want to determine the reasons for such slippages. Such instances of poor project control can increase costs substantially.

OPERATION COSTS

To get an accurate picture of the cost of a hardware acquisition project, the auditor must look at the operation costs. If this is not done, *changes* in lease cost, personnel cost, and the like should be figured over some reasonable period of time (e.g., one to three years) so that these cost changes can be figured into the acquisition costs. A better approach, however, is to divide costs into one-time costs (i.e., the acquisition costs) and recurring costs (i.e., the operation costs).

The costs over several months should be averaged to determine a typical month's operation costs. This helps to eliminate the effect of seasonal changes (i.e., abnormally high- or abnormally low-cost months). The minimum period used should be three months—hence the recommendation to do the audit no sooner than three months after project completion.

The recurring costs associated with operating computers and computer-related equipment can be grouped into the following areas:
- Facilities costs
- Hardware and communications costs
- Supplies and miscellaneous costs
- Personnel costs

Although not all operation costs apply to every equipment project, a comprehensive checklist of operation costs is given in this section.

The auditor should attempt to determine both the gross costs and the net change in costs for each item on the schedule; it is the net change in costs that measures the impact of the new equipment. If the net change results in less cost, the savings should be included on the Quantified Benefits Schedule, whether or not such savings were anticipated.

Facilities Costs

If the organization does not allocate facilities costs to departments, these costs may have to be estimated based on the number of square feet occupied by the DP organization. The following costs generally apply only when major

changes in equipment occur:
- Depreciation, lease, or rental of the building space devoted to the equipment, the tape library, and the support equipment (e.g., bursters, decollators). If this is a first-time computer installation, space for data-entry personnel, programmers, and DP management should also be included.
- Property tax on the space used.
- Property insurance on the space used.
- Utilities costs, including water, electricity, heat, and telephone for those lines and telephones not used for data communications.
- Depreciation, lease, or rental of off-site storage space.
- Transportation to the off-site storage space.
- Fees paid to ensure a backup operation site for use should a disaster occur.

Hardware and Communications Costs

The following hardware and communications costs should be included:
- Depreciation, lease, or rental of the computer mainframe.
- Depreciation, lease, or rental of the peripherals—It may be desirable to list separately such items as disk drives, tape drives, card readers and punches, and printers.
- Depreciation, lease, or rental of remote terminals, including CRTs, keyboard devices, printers, and RJE equipment.
- Depreciation, lease, or rental of communications equipment, including data phones, modems, multiplexors, concentrators, front-end computers, microwave systems; the cost of leased lines; and dial-up charges associated with data transmission.
- Monthly maintenance costs (if not included in the lease or rental costs)—The charges for off-hours maintenance should also be included.
- Use tax (if not included in the lease or rental costs)—In some instances, the state may present a semiannual bill for use tax rather than having the vendor add it to the monthly billing.
- Property tax (if not included in the lease or rental costs)—Who must pay this cost is usually spelled out in the contract.
- Property insurance on the equipment—Who must carry this insurance is also usually in the contract. The auditor may find that the lessor is responsible for this insurance but that it is not being carried. Such situations should be brought to the attention of management.
- Amortization, lease, or rental of software for the equipment, including operating systems and communications monitors—Applications packages and other software (e.g., a data base management system) that might be authorized in a separate project should be excluded.

Supplies and Miscellaneous Costs

The following supplies and miscellaneous costs should also be recorded:
- Disk pack rental or depreciation or costs for disk packs that are pur-

chased and expensed
- The costs of tapes, disks, diskettes, and/or cartridges that are purchased and expensed
- The cost of punched cards used each month
- The cost of preprinted computer forms that are used each month
- The cost of stock computer paper used each month
- Printer ribbons and keypunch equipment costs
- The cost of miscellaneous supplies (e.g., toner for computer-connected reproduction equipment, film for COM equipment, ink for ink-jet printers and plotters, tape seals for filing reels of tape, and cleaning supplies to clean tape heads)
- The cost of outside data-entry vendors regularly used in lieu of, or to supplement, in-house capability
- The cost of various types of insurance, including business interruption, valuable papers, media, extra expense, and liability

Personnel Costs

These costs should include salaries and wages as well as benefits and, where appropriate, burden, general, and administrative overhead allowances. It is advisable that each of these types of costs be shown separately since benefits and overhead may be overlooked when the equipment proposal is prepared. Not all of the following functional groupings apply in every instance:

- DP management, supervisors, and administrative personnel (e.g., secretaries and documentation writers).
- Security officers and data base administration staff.
- Systems analysts and application programmers.
- Software programmers.
- Computer and RJE operators.
- Control and support personnel (e.g., burster operators, tape librarians, delivery persons).
- Data-entry personnel.
- Guards, janitors, and maintenance personnel. If they are not employees, fees paid to agencies should be recorded.
- User personnel, where appropriate. Such costs should be included, for example, when CRTs are placed in user departments and thus the data-entry function is transferred from the data-entry group to user personnel. If possible, user personnel costs should be shown by department.

QUANTIFIED BENEFITS

By determining the net change in operation costs, the auditor will detect many benefits achieved; planned benefits that were not obtained will also come to light. Because staff reductions (a frequent benefit) cannot occur as soon as the equipment becomes operational, there is usually a timetable for achieving anticipated benefits.

HARDWARE COST/BENEFIT REVIEW

When the time from planning to evaluating is fairly long, the effects of inflation should be considered. For example, after a personnel reduction, there may be little difference between the total "after" salaries and the total "before" salaries because of an intervening cost-of-living adjustment. This might seem to indicate that the planned benefit was not achieved. If, however, the number of reductions is multiplied by the average "after" salary, it might indicate that the benefit was more than attained. The auditor must determine how to present the fairest picture.

Some quantifiable, but not quantified, benefits can be listed. For example, the proposal might say that "the equipment will result in less downtime" without specifying a criterion for judging "less" and without indicating the current amount of downtime. In such instances, the auditor should attempt to determine the initial value of the measure that was to be improved and the values for that measure at the time of the audit. In this way, actual values can be used to determine whether benefits were achieved.

Equipment change proposals generally list two types of quantified benefits—those to which a dollar value has been assigned and those without a dollar value (e.g., personnel reductions, reduction in equipment downtime, increased processing speeds). Although it is difficult to develop a comprehensive list of quantified benefits, the following provides a starting point.

Monetary Savings

Monetary savings fit within the following categories:
- Reduction in wages, salaries, fringe benefits, and overhead resulting from personnel reductions—In evaluating whether this benefit is achieved, transfers to other departments should not be considered as cost reduction. Furthermore, any reductions should be offset by salary increases resulting from an upgrading in job level. Upgrading is a common practice when people who were doing a manual, clerical job are retrained to use CRTs.
- Reduction in wages, salaries, and fringe benefits resulting from job-level downgrading—Such savings can be theoretical or deferred. If a job is downgraded without a corresponding wage cut, savings are realized only when an employee leaves and is replaced by a new hire.
- Staff avoidance savings—This is another type of theoretical saving whose achievement is difficult to determine. Factors other than new or changed equipment can result in staff avoidance (e.g., decreases in sales or transfers of functions to other departments). The auditor may want to give credit for staff avoidance only if a measure of productivity that substantiates the claim can be established. If an employee who processed 100 transactions per day prior to the change afterward processes 150, for example, the claim of staff avoidance would seem to be justified.
- Reduction in processing costs—This is another benefit that is hard to pin down. Reductions can result from programming changes, from the mix of applications being run, or because of improved manual proce-

dures that have nothing to do with the equipment change. If everything remains constant except the hardware, and costs go down, it is safe to conclude that processing costs were reduced.
- Reduction in equipment rentals—The realization of this benefit is easy to determine, but price increases or decreases can have an effect and should be considered.
- Avoidance of equipment rentals—Determining whether this benefit was achieved presents many of the same problems as does staff avoidance savings. Here again, the auditor should look for "before" and "after" measures of productivity.
- Reduction in facilities costs (e.g., those for floor space, electricity, and communications)—Comparing "before" and "after" invoices is probably the best approach to use in evaluating this benefit. If a new computer uses 200 fewer square feet of space but this space is unusable by any other organization for security reasons, the benefit has not been achieved.
- Avoidance of facilities costs—This benefit can be claimed only if adding staff or equipment is avoided and if it would have been necessary to increase the floor space had the staff or equipment been added.
- Reduction in maintenance costs—A comparison of "before" and "after" invoices should determine whether maintenance costs were reduced.
- Reduction in the cost of supplies—Such benefits are often claimed when an organization changes from keypunch to key-to-disk data entry or from centralized data entry to CRTs located in user areas. In some cases, the change represents a replacement of one type of supply by another (e.g., tapes and/or disks for punch cards). In such cases, the net saving should be used.

Nonmonetary Savings

Proposals for equipment changes may promise some of the following:
- Reduction in personnel—Savings here are in salaries, wages, and benefits. To give credit for both personnel and salary savings would be to give double credit for a single achievement.
- Increased production per employee—This benefit is directly related to staff avoidance savings and salary savings. Again, the auditor should be cautioned about giving double credit for a single achievement.
- Improved accuracy—It may be difficult to get statistics to substantiate this type of claim.
- Reduced turnaround time for processing a transaction.
- Lower employee turnover rate because of improved morale—Of the many reasons that people leave a company, the computer equipment used is only one. Although people in the DP industry like to work with the latest equipment, the impact on turnover is hard to judge.
- Faster processing based on equipment specifications.

Effect of Schedule Slippage

When the equipment implementation schedule slips, the achievement of benefits is affected. If staff reductions or realignments in user organizations are involved, slippages can delay benefits and can also result in increased costs. In addition, rumors of personnel changes resulting from equipment changes cannot be suppressed, and undue delays can make user personnel anxious. The result can be unrest, poor morale, and, in the worst case, the best people (who find it easiest to get other jobs) may leave. These are hidden costs that offset benefits but are probably not measurable.

Another possible effect of schedule slippage is lengthening of the schedule for achieving benefits. For example, instead of the anticipated benefits being planned for within one year of the equipment change, the plan may be formally or informally extended to 18 months.

A third possible effect is that schedule slippages result in lost benefits that can never be recovered. If a staff reduction is delayed by six months, for example, those six months of salary savings are lost forever. This should be emphasized in the audit report.

The following nonquantified benefits are typical:
- Improved morale.
- Improved customer relations.
- Improved company image.
- Faster turnaround of transactions. If possible, this should be quantified by the auditor, even if it was not quantified in the supporting documents.
- More timely information.
- Improved controls.
- Greater flexibility in handling data.
- Greater productivity. Again, this should be measured if possible.
- Change from outdated to current technology.

Because of the nature of nonquantified benefits, it is hard to determine whether they have been achieved or not. Judgment rather than evaluation of objective data is required. The auditor can use the techniques of interviewing, reviewing, and observing in this effort. Whether each nonquantified benefit was achieved, not achieved, or partially achieved can then be recorded.

A questionnaire based on the items in the Nonquantified Benefits Schedule can be very useful. Users and DP personnel who might benefit from or be affected by the equipment change should be interviewed to see whether, in their opinion, specific benefits were attained. Two questions that should be on the bottom of the questionnaire are, Were there any other benefits resulting from the new equipment that you haven't told me about yet? and Were there any unexpected problems?

If better data or reports are to be a benefit, the auditor should review the "before" and "after" reports and judge whether they are improved. If so, it must be determined whether the improvements resulted from the equipment or from programming changes. In addition, the auditor should observe the processing to determine how the equipment has affected controls and the timeliness of reports.

THE AUDIT REPORT

The audit report should indicate all significant variances from plans in installation costs, operation costs, quantified benefits achieved, and nonquantified benefits achieved. Where reasons for variances can be determined, these should be indicated. In some cases, steps can be taken to improve unfavorable variances, particularly with regard to reducing operating costs and obtaining more benefits; these steps should be recommended.

During the course of the study, the auditor may find that there are major difficulties with the equipment. All such cases should be pointed out, together with any recommendations for improvement.

Although this is not intended to be an audit of controls and procedures, some problems may come to light. These, of course, should be noted on the audit report, particularly variations that adversely affect controls, costs, or system performance. An audit of this type discloses how well the project control system is operating.

CONCLUSION

When management (or audit committee) approval has been obtained, a hardware acquisition cost/benefit review work program based on the material in this chapter can be developed. By following the work program, the auditor can uncover areas in which large cost savings can be achieved through improved management monitoring and better project control procedures. The process of authorizing projects can then be refined as experience is gained in this area. Audits of this type allow the EDP auditor to help achieve cost savings and increased cost benefits for the organization.